The Heart of a Humble Wildflower

Sarai Saporta

Table of Contents

When I first looked into my parent's effects and found their writings, I knew that the treasure I had found would bring back a lot of memories and most of them were confusing and sometimes unpleasant. Of course, my brother and I had the usual boyhood found in the places we moved to back east in the early '60s and '70s. And since my father and mother were freely active in social movements to bring in social change, we had the opportunity to meet unusual college students, artists, and thinkers who later on came to influence the world we know today. Back then, for two boys who were interested in play and sometimes did not give thought to their recklessness or the physical consequences or the parental punishments that would occur later on an almost routine frequency. For example:

Batman and Robin

My earliest memory was of playing Batman and my brother who played Robin – in our underwear and with bath towels wrapped around our necks - for cloaks. We were living in the big Ashburn Road house in Pennsylvania, it was a great place for two young children to grow up. It was a large two-story with a large attic that was really a finished attic with two more rooms, and we had a basement to go exploring in. If that wasn't enough, we had a huge backyard and a front yard complete with a tire swing. And if that wasn't enough, just down the street was a stand of trees reminiscent of an old forest, complete with old leaves from countless falls and the smell of freshness. Who could want anything more?

My brother and I were playing batman and robin, the Ashburn road house had two sets of stairs one in the front with a grand banister and one in the back which led to the kitchen and the basement where we kept the washer and dryer and the painting and turpentine my mother used when she wanted to paint. This information would become significant later as my brother found some used turpentine there, thought it was milk (it looked white), and drank it.

My brother and I loved to slide down the front stairs grand banister and we did this often, yelling and screaming and having a great time, always managing to get off in time before the other brother came careening onto the place where the other had just recently vacated.

As we were fighting crime with "truth and justice," I was the first to reach the banister of bliss and slide down it as fast as I could, after the bad guy. My cape whipped around me and my legs hiked up high to get as much speed as I could. And there was my brother close behind me. We had done this four or five times in dedicated succession, I remember being out of breath and hitting the bottom post. As I paused briefly before getting off to catch my breath, my brother came down almost on top of me.

As I ran down the hall to go to the kitchen staircase I thought my brother was closely following behind me to continue the fun. I heard a loud crash and a loud howl behind me, I wheeled around and ran back to see what the matter was, my mother got there before me – I don't know how. And there was my brother, Joe, howling on the tile floor, he had fallen off the banister from the wrong side and the drop was a lot more than he had anticipated.

As my mother and by this time, my father had arrived from where he was in the upstairs attic room studio (where he created the sound sculpture with Rob Goodman): they discussed whether they should call the doctor. This was the time before they invented HMOs and in those days doctors made house calls. My brother and I both hated to see the doctor because the visit there always involved getting a shot of some kind. My brother was limping around saying "see – I can walk, I don't need to see the doctor." After appraising the situation critically, my mother called Doctor Barolle and after a brief conversation took my brother to meet him at the hospital. I stayed home with my dad.

A short time later, my mother and brother arrived and I remember my father having to carry my brother up to his room. Why? You may ask. The doctor knowing our family well and specifically my brother's active spirit had prepared a special cast for him. It was a huge body cast that came up to his chest! The doctor thought it was best if he immobilized Joe until he healed from the hairline fracture. I think my brother called it a compound fracture but I remember later that mom called it a hairline fracture.

And there my brother stayed for six months until he completely healed. I remember I had to go to school and bring his homework to him. The homework wasn't much because I was still in the first grade and Joe was still in kindergarten. I still remember drawing a picture of the Mayflower for school and my brother was very impressed. I am sure it was hard on my parents because they had to watch over him and make sure he got fed and cleaned. I'll never forget the look of fear on my brother's face when I ran up to him. Nor the look of anger and then concern on my mother's when she called and notified the doctor of the situation.

However, what would also occur later in my life, now that I am sixty, is that I realized I really didn't know my parents nearly as well as I thought I did.

Heart of the Universe

My mother wrote this poem with her new computer in 1992:

> Made Wise by the encounter
> Between
> Misery and
> Splendor
> I am the Heart of a hum
> ble
> Wildflower
> Taking its stand
> In
> The
> Heart of the
> UNIVERSE

However, the above barely reveals the strength of the poem, so I have included the actual page with the imagery done in her version of a computer-driven poem.

Made *Wise* by the encounter

between

misery and

Splendor
I am the *Heart* of a *hum*
ble

WILDFLOWER

taking its stand

in

the

heart of the

UNIVERSE

After years of putting her desire to paint on the back burner, raising children, and trying to understand the world. The seed that was held back began to break through the ice and stone of the years.

All families struggle and with the threat of poverty, social problems that lead to isolation, and safe places to live are a challenge to find, not to mention finding a fulfilling spiritual understanding. I didn't even know I was Jewish until I was six years old. These problems were always in the background when my brother and I grew up.   It was present with the suburbia of Elkin's Park, the restlessness of Bleecker Street in New York, and the unforgiving New Mexico environment and the local people at the time.

It wasn't that I had bitter, understating, anger towards these places, it was that my anger was constantly being fed by a variety of reasons both rooted in family and social adjustments that I was constantly being forced into as my parents moved from place to place. I believe military children would understand the relentless feeling inside that I am describing.

We were all getting the feelings and expressing them in our own way of understanding. My brother left for Arizona when he was 16. I myself felt cheated because I stayed on and went to college without a clear direction of why I wanted to be in college. My father continued his quest to understand his art through the Kototama understanding of the nature of the universe and in part isolated from the rest of the family. My mother seemed to be the most adjusted, being the secretary for her spiritual teacher. The teacher who she adored, the reason why we moved the New Mexico, the fountain of wisdom, and the master pioneer.

Much later, after my father died and I was married with a child on the way, and my brother settled in Seattle, Washington and married, did the anger she was feeling come out.

She writes:

Stepping Stones on the Decisions to Move Again

1. HKL [the short name she gave her husband HiKaLu a.k.a. Carl Fernbach-Flarsheim] dies and I am bereft and relieved at the same time.
2. I need to live quietly, introspectively, to lick my wounds and learn my lessons. To understand what led me to being such a martyr and how to recover.
3. Grief passes, slowly in stages, and I am prone present for myself, at the moment.
4. I realize I have woven a cocoon around myself and it is time to come out.
5. But not here, to leave the past behind, to unloosen the bonds. I must go to another place. There's still too much here to keep me enclosed.

6. It's time to expand – in Seattle, it seems where. My son welcomes me. It seems pretty open, psychically.

7. Two weeks to departure. So many kind friends making gestures of the ritual of good-bye. To see me once more before I go, to wish me well.

8. I didn't want to lose my courage, thinking about all this. Thought muddles action – but this close, it's ok – and very soothing to my inner being.

9. Still working on the PageMaker project, until the end – drop caps, Bodoni book, double spaced, etc. Why am I helpless with this marvelous toy – everything is just energy on a screen. No form, like a priori energy and then creating my manifestation in the physical world called 'heard copy.' Getting to know Joe again [my brother, Joe Farbrook], as he is now, and his wife, and my grandson. The interaction between family again. Time for me to practice having healthier relationships, now that I've the insight about fear and control. If a decision is right, it progresses on all levels at once.

10. And David, will he grow up, now that I'll be gone, and deal with reality instead of projected fantasy. Not just losing himself in his work and letting his life slip by? I know he'll be well and strong and it feels right.

11. I feel mostly determined to put it all behind me and glad form my decision to begin again, with love and gratitude for the person I've become now. And whatever lies ahead.

This sounds all very intelligent and in facing the prospects of a huge move after the recent death of her husband, she was in many ways standing alone. She couldn't escape from the truth though. She felt that inner abandonment heard it as an inner whisper. How will you know? Can you save yourself from yourself? Can you understand that rejecting the world is a part of the fear that you have hidden all along since being very young? She began by joining a support group of others who had recently been involved with a loss of a loved one. She later writes:

Reaction to reading it aloud to others (Penny and Doris):

I'm having difficulty breathing – what are they thinking of what I said? Now that I've got my thoughts and feelings out – is it ok? Am I too weird to be acceptable? There's always this little critical voice inside, angry with me for breaking the mold that I was supposed to be molded into. That's the past, nothing to do with present healing. I don't have to be burdened with what no longer exists – only in distant memory.

I am alright to be who I am. I can be confident and enjoy those things I love to do freely. No one's going to be mad at me. That died long ago. I am capable of having my own life, shaping it into what's appropriate and satisfying to my inner self. That kind of life is what's worthwhile, worth living for. I pray for loving guidance – to assuage that criticizing, self-hating voice. I love her, too. She needn't be afraid of what she doesn't understand. I understand and she'll be safe with me.

We are here in this space, continued by our limitations, to search for the self. There's nothing more valuable than that. And to help others to do the same whenever possible. To get beyond the denials to a bigger universe.

I keep seeing the horizon, by daytime and by night. A distant plain to journey through, live with no idea what the reality will be there. I try not to fantasize but I keep catching myself, making assumptions and lots of wishful thinking that everything will be better there. But it is always I that is wherever there is – it's not breaking off so much as a contamination of the I. But with more space to maneuver, more opportunities to keep going. A more benign place? No, just the next place where I need to be. If I flower, I'll call it benign. If I can be of use, to myself and to others, I'll say it's fulfilling. But that's where I need to be now.

And what of the losses? I'm leaving behind – like the power of the mountains, they said goodbye to me with a rainbow. Is anything ever really lost? Just put back in the box like outgrown toys. I'll see what toys appear in the next place, to help me negotiate the next coming phase. I kiss each toy as I put them away; I welcome the new ones, grateful as they appear. I'm waxing sentimental, it's these mixed with the determination and spirit of adventure, too.

And how I thought Penny was trying to humiliate me by suggesting we meet at my taken apart house – what paranoia! It was a mature, loving session.

This is a story of personal revelation that only being in this world for sixty years can bring. It seems that it takes this kind of time and experience to examine the possibilities and understand the references we placed on ourselves from childhood from the perspective of culture, society of the times, and family. An inheritance that could be good or not but is an examination of change where we decide whether the ghosts we lived with are still relevant or not. Certain things I would say help carry us over the hurdles of life's obstacles and our objectivity. But if you are no longer "breathing" because you are someone you yourself would not want to talk to? Hello?

What do you surrender to? Who do you become after the fall of the ideals and things you trusted in the past? The fix is not simple when you tell yourself you are not broken but that everybody else is. Do you go on sleeping away from your life and relive the yesterdays of glory and regret?

Are you beginning to understand my question? Who are my parents, who is this person that was my mother? She was a caregiver and someone to get angry at when my most precious desire was to stop the pain of being a child and move into adulthood. But before I was born, and after I left the house?

The journey I am proposing is of one person who found that there was more to life than self-sacrifice and being so intense that no one could hold a conversation with her long enough to get to the conclusion. The next chapter begins an intimate journey of an artist that was more than just a person following the ghosts of her monsters and past memories.

Life is brutal, but through the challenges there came a flower that slowly evolved into a complete human being. When I got through the personal challenges of re-experiencing my life with her through my lens, I realized this was a sensitive portrayal of a person who took the time to write about her life in a personal and intimate way, and more importantly, was able to write about it as an invitation to her personal world.

Something awaits for you, too.

Can you hear me?

On Going Under, Defects, and Dependency

The moral origin of all genuine politics.. living truth.. in the last analysis, it is not power that matters but values.. decency, reason, responsibility, civility, and tolerance.. defining the basics of liberty.

- Valdav Havel

July 9, 1992. To remember that I'm a lovable person whatever my shortcomings; in self-love, I am free to let go of my shortcomings. It's only when I feel inadequate and unworthy do I revert to my compulsive behavior, and feel miserable, twisted, and out of sync with the universe. Criticizing myself only leaves me as less. Only as I am, my natural self, will my shortcomings like a virus, leave me and find no home to thrive in.

My character defects come out of my self-hate when nothing I do is ever good enough nor is who I am good enough. That's this society's plan, not mine. I don't have to be a slave or a robot to an authoritarian society, internalized through the generations that only wants control, and power over me, not what's good or right for me.

It is this society that is immoral and renders me less than my fully human self. In order to change it and bring peace, and natural order between people, I begin with myself, and pray for the insight and courage it takes to affirm my natural being, precious and free.

As a student of the truth, I am not concerned with the material game which uses the acquisition of things and outside opinion as to the basis of self-esteem. I esteem myself as one who is searching for the truth. I can't help it; it's a necessity that drives me on. Nothing else gives me such great pleasure and a sense of meaning to my life as when I discover another technique I've been unconsciously using to plague myself with self-doubt.

Clearly, I need to let go of one dirty trick after another on my path of truth-seeking. I don't need to get sucked in by the attitudes of those people in denial even though they're in the majority and some of whom are the people I love. They are none of them my guides.

I listen inside and go my way.

June 10, 1992. With each painful encounter with my feelings of unworthiness, I now have the ability, by grace, to stop and think it over more rationally. I grew up in a situation where impossible and inconsistent demands were made of me which made me feel angry and victimized. Which I was.

But my life is in my own hands now and I don't have to demand the impossible from myself and I don't have to feel defensive about it. If my love is not good enough, I don't have to feel ashamed and over-compensate by giving too much. What love I have is all I have and I need to love myself first.

I would like to feel myself a worthy human being, not having to compulsively be performing miracles. That I can accept my shortcomings as part of being a worthy person anyway. It's egomania to think I can do it all by myself. May I have the patience and confidence to work through the process of re-gaining my self-esteem a little at a time. Happening of itself. Falling into doubt is not a loving thing to do to myself and I don't have to. My higher self knows better and I deserve the joy and peace, certain that things will work out as they should. Even unfortunate events have their good side that I can benefit from.

Removing my shortcomings means having the ability to keep my faith – to keep connected with reality. Only when I feel dark and anxious do I exhibit my compulsive, self-destructive behavior, feeling I don't love enough and don't deserve to be loved. No one can love that much and it's not necessary to. I don't have to be so heroic. That's unreal.

Peace and happiness is when I'm confidently connected with my truth and from there, all peace flows outward to the others. I needn't throw my life away like it's worthless to prove my worth. How contradictory, but there it is. May I stay connected and learn from when I'm not.

July 19, 1992 from Dōgen

> Refrain from unwholesome actions
> Not attached to birth and death
> Compassionate to all sentient beings
> Respectful to seniors and kind to juniors
> Not excluding or desiring anything, with no designing thoughts
> or worries
> You will be called a Buddha
> Do not seek anything else.
> Not consciousness but merging with realization.
> There is something free from all of these understandings.
> Water's freedom depends only on water. Take up water and
> make it your body and mind, make it your thought.

From Confucius

> I do not mind not being in office. All I mind about is whether I have the
> qualities that entitle me to office.
> I do not mind failing to get recognition. I am too busy doing the things that
> entitle me to recognition.

July 22, 1992. Humbly asked God to remove my shortcomings to see things as they are. To relieve me of the burden of the past. Still in bondage to the one I trust and believe in. He lashed out at me again and I experienced great physical as well as mental pain. I was able to get out of the most sensational symptoms in a few hours, a much shorter time than I would have in the past but the darkness in my mind continued to linger for another painful week. It was a struggle to re-establish my present reality rather than relive a painful, childhood past of humiliation and degradation. Inside I still hate myself, something internalized from the emotional neglect I had been subjected to.

When I'm attacked today, I respond as if that's exactly the way I deserve to be treated and I live out the past again, out of all proportion with the present. I am always a victim, identifying with my exploiters. I want to die or throw out everything and run away. I'm not responsible for other people's cruelty because they are disappointed or frustrated, using me as a scapegoat. I need to be more detached, to accept their temporary insanity which I don't have to deal with as my own. But that's so difficult when I'm already poisoned by self-hate, bringing the past into the present and setting myself up at the least opportunity.

My father was always angry and lashing out at me when I was just becoming sexually mature. He would insult and humiliate me in front of other people, using me for his ego and not caring how I was being wounded. And yet he was secretly proud of me, I know. I relive those teenage years of emptiness and confusion with this present person. I mistake him for my father. I don't understand him or see him realistically. I don't know who he is. I think if I could see him in his reality I would understand myself. But I keep getting in my own way, carrying the past and making him some sort of hero, holding up a false mirror.

As my spiritual guide, I hunger for even the few precious crumbs he doles out to me. I become stupid when I want to ask for more, afraid of his demeaning, humiliating replies. If I could only get in touch with my self-love, buried deep inside, I would not be reacting deja vue. I would good-naturedly understand his bad temper and frustration in not being able to turn out better students who could understand his message. I doggedly stick with him as my only hope in a hopeless world. I'm my own obstruction because of my self-hate. But I shall flower in my own time. Can I ever be entirely honest with him and tell him my truth, being entirely present, whatever his reaction? I ask that this self-hate be removed from me by the judgment of my inner love.

Obsessing on the outcome, a happier future, I am paralyzed in the present. I am vulnerable to emotional blackmail, the way HKL used pity to keep me with him, as a victim. The way out of the dilemma is through self-love. The judgment that regards me as unique and precious, guiding me to freedom.

August 5, 1992. To be able to stand on my own and then make friends, and be able to ask for help as well. I sit in splendid isolation, heavy with pride and the fear of being rejected. I'd like to be easier with myself and not overreact. That means self-forgiveness, having my self-hate be removed from me. Now that I'm in touch with it. I can more easily accept people as they are, instead of re-creating them to suit my needs. I'm thinking of starting over again. In Seattle? Because Joe's there; I'll know somebody.

Santa Fe is ok but it's become too heavy. There's a pall hanging over me here, where I spent so much time in misery and plain torture. I can never be the person I was before all this. Changing my environment will release all the old stuff and let me act with the present. Here in Seattle, I'm in transition but I can see I've changed and am feeling more of a sense of self.

I would like to be treating more patients; maybe it's the economy that's so difficult. The nation, the world, it seems everything is down and I can barely make the effort to do anything on the outside. I was so frightened to do even small things like selling out my herbs and Sensei's latest book. But I started thinking about leaving and it gave me the impetus to go out there and not care so much who rejects me. Then I heard it. Sensei's loving voice and I almost changed my mind. But I really should unshackle myself from my emotional dependency on him and his on me. It's so limited on that level. I don't know how he will react (on the outside), he will probably not want to interfere. And how will Joe and Marcelle feel? We all need our own space. And how will Dave feel inside? But we're all grownups now and maybe it will be a good thing.

I feel I am hiding from the world, and I would like to be out there, involved as a healer. Seattle's a bigger, richer town but I would need to connect with people. There are so few even here that I can talk Kototama to. But there's CoDA and they're also in Seattle. I hope it won't be hard to maintain my spiritual practice alone there but here my life is too one-sided and overly concentrated. I need to expand my horizons and meet new challenges with courage and confidence. Practicing my self-esteem has really been taking a drubbing these last ten years. Actually, it's been so much longer. I remember all the miserable years with HKL even before he got sick and became such a dictator.

We will see if, by October, my practice doesn't improve, I will rent out the house and take off in May. Was this my original plan? It's hard to remember, it's changed so. I need to be this great Mother, I wonder if my sons had to hide their imperfections and fears from me so I wouldn't be hurt. My feelings and self-image, perhaps my children recognized my neediness.

Part of the History of the House

August 28, 1992. I am a part of the history of this house, now. The changes I made, the peculiarities made for forgotten purposes then but no longer needed, now. How important, crucial actually, they seemed then, the twenty years of living here, the details hardly remembered. But leaving their ghosts as part of the fabric of the place. My spirit, my joy and suffering, the discoveries and inner changes, too. All passing now but leaving its mark, same vibrations behind. HKL is gone, now. Thank God. But he visits me sometimes and lets me know how very well he is, showing me in an inner golden glow that I can feel intuitively, more than see.

There are traces of all the children, as they were growing up, and something of the cats, and the dogs. These are left behind and something of myself. Redeemed and leaving now that the work is gone. The required transformations and the results I carry with me. What new spirit will live here now? The events of another life to come will add themselves to the fabric of this house.

August 29, 1992. I caught myself this morning. There is a part of me that's afraid when patients come. That I will fail or make a mistake, it's almost as if I'm supposed to. I remember having bizarre dreams like that. It's something inside of me, how I forget my successes, the triumphs of good work. I almost did make a mistake yesterday which I rectified. I struggled not to bash myself about it, asking to be a victim. I'm trying to understand David doing the same with his wife. She is a greedy child, trying to rip me off and he's angry with me for not allowing it, the way he does. He feels he can never be good enough and she uses it to control him.

June 1, 1992. His devil-spirit stimulated all my inner resources, the ones I didn't know were there. In the end, it strengthened me, and maybe that's why I had to go through all that misery and pain. I've come out quite a different person. More sure of the necessity of pursuing my real path, finding out who I really am. It would be impossible for me to choose to do such a thing again. Abandoning this real self because I hadn't valued it enough in opposition to what was imposed on me by family and society.

June 4, 1992. One of the unexpected benefits of living a solitary life is how important each visitor or phone call becomes. Each encounter becomes a unique experience, savored and remembered with a depth unimaginable when it's just one more event amidst family, guests, etc. The debris of many cares, solutions, aspirations has all been cleared away and I can see each one better. In its own light.

June 8, 1992. Yesterday, I was lost in the woods, my car in a ditch, alone, raining, not the right shoes. But I didn't fall down into fear; I didn't have to play the panicky, frightened woman role – like having taken off clothes that didn't fit me. Tonight, I realized that if someone sincerely loved me, I'd be sick with fear and really lose it. I asked myself why, and what came back in response was guilt. I didn't know how to really love anyone. I can just keep giving excessively of myself but I don't know about love. This is what I've been avoiding looking at.

I had been stuffing it all down. I can't give or receive real love. But I'm still ok. I don't have to be better than who I am.. right now. When I was very young, I would sit on my mother's lap, where she would treat me like I was her favorite doll. I remember my mother telling me, how much she loved me. Her love was very grandiose but also very exclusive, she was the only one who could love like that. I should treasure her as a rare and fixate only on her. Maybe that's how I began feeling so guilty and not wanting to be loved so much like that. I was expected to let her consume me and never separate to have my own life. I was being suffocated and by age three I had climbed down off her lap and refused her adoration, anymore.

In reality, love has many splendors, and perfect love is an ideal. I don't have to be afraid that I don't deserve such splendor. It was her fantasy and I can give it back to her.

June 11, 1992. I don't have to be afraid of being sincerely loved because that kind of love doesn't need to consume me. I don't have to run for my life. I was afraid to be loved because it meant dying for my authentic self. I can sincerely love without losing myself, I can keep what is mine. I don't have to compensate for my inadequacies by giving it all away. I can keep my power and love gently, the passion within bounds. Romantic love is fantasy, full of mirrors and projections. The real person is lost in the dark woods. For that, I am not responsible.

June 9, 1992. Meditation, how easily I can lose it. My self-confidence was destroyed by my fear. So, I pick up the pieces and try again to regain my lost peace of mind. I can't be shackled by old mistakes, old seductions that I succumbed to. I have the present, my present life to live, this day and minute. I cannot allow the pressures put on me by others to rob me of this, my present. I can keep faith and trust what my inner knowing tells me. I might be wishfully thinking at times, and I try to force it. What my voice is telling me. If I am not right, I will find out and I won't be destroyed because of it. I'm allowed to be mistaken. The only mistake would be to give it up and fall back into darkness. I forgave myself when I lose my faith and let doubt put my light into shadow. It's not so important to be right but rather to have light – to be light.

I have a choice to be joyfully at one with the universe or to worry about the lack of money. My inability to earn it, and how will I pay the bills. So many small miracles have occurred on that score. I didn't know I could receive a widow's pension at my present age. I was feeling too proud to inquire, but when I had to, I was so grateful that it was there for me. To help me recover until I could make my own way again – or not. I am free to continue this interior life I'm pursuing wherever it will take me. I don't have to find some other menial job. I can wait until the patients start coming again. With my faith and trust, and with confidence in my abilities to help people in a meaningful way. I gave all my power to a dying man. It was ill-advised but also because I was afraid of social disapproval, and to nurture myself. A wife to abandon her husband in sickness, I couldn't rationalize it away. I had to give him all of myself until I had nothing left. But I also know about loving someone, now. That I don't really love someone when I give everything away. I can distinguish between loving and giving. Giving because I feel worthless and can never give adequately enough. This is a lack of self-love, of abandoning myself. I can love without losing myself, accepting the limitations of what is possible, and reconciling myself to the inevitable end of a hopeless illness, in this case.

To destroy me is a lack of love and giving in to the fear that I'm not good enough to have a life. This is unreasonable, not love. Had I been able to understand about loving him and myself, I could have let him go sooner, let him die peacefully. Even discussed it with him realistically but both of us were frightened children in the dark woods, holding each other's hand.

I don't have to feel ashamed of all this. It's what this society teaches us to do. Let the rules control us rather than my own good sense. When I allow myself to be controlled from the outside, by the rules that I internalized in childhood, then I am only a robot not a human being. I become someone's computer, someone I never met and who doesn't know me either. I give myself permission to find my real self and to get out of being controlled. It is I who am ultimately I control, I just have to find my knowing inner voice and follow its direction. This is being free. This opens up all kinds of possibilities that are waiting for me to try them. This is my real inheritance. The truth of my present life in this time and place.

I feel happy because I choose to be. I choose to stay in direct connection with the universe which is who I am. For that, I will take responsibility. I cannot control what other people do, they have their own way to go and it is not my work to interfere. I can only be a light for others to see if they wish. I feel grateful that I'm finding all this now because it wasn't possible before and everything that went before has led me to this. I am learning my way. I live in the now. No other place is real existence. I feel I'm coming out from behind a cloud, not of my own making so much as one I cooperated with. Not is the time for consciousness.

It takes courage to get beyond the program into full humanness but that is my journey. The culmination of past experiences, and what I can understand now. For each moment of sanity, I am strengthened to continue this journey. For each moment of doubt and darkness, I am giving myself a lesson. I don't have to hide from the pain of it. With each release back into sanity, I am that much more whole and knowledgeable of the way to go.

July 11, 1992. I dreamt of an old idea. I needed to please my father (distant man that he was) as well as my first husband (also a distant man). I have two men to please. And the father was complaining, he felt he should be the only one to please. Perhaps, I thought being in a hopeless marriage (to Ted) was appeasement. That first week of my marriage (I still remember it), I dreamt I was covered in mud from the beach and the tide that was coming up very quickly. I got my white dress dirty. The ocean kept drenching me and I couldn't avoid it.

Looking at it now, I was not being true to myself. I was covering myself in the mud as a way to hide my true self. Which I felt was unacceptable and I needed to survive with my true self somehow intact. I was protecting myself under the camouflage of ocean and sand. It has to be sand because it was so sterile, a commentary on the role I felt obliged to play. When I married, my family could no longer pressure me and manipulate me into becoming their creature. Oh, what I know now, I needn't have felt so guilty about what I did. This dream has remained with me all this time, like a seed of understanding waiting for the right conditions in which to sprout.

And along came Furiya, a man I came to know while I was still married to Ted, he hadn't come back to town yet and delayed as much as he could. I ate up Furiya's affection. But who knows. I couldn't accept love in those days and it would have gone rotten sooner or later. The relationship was bound to fail. So I treasure the good moments we had together. It's been laying there such a long time and just now I am remembering it. I'm sure he never suspected.

I must have an affinity for the Japanese. They keep appearing in my life, always in a good, and important way. Helping me along. Like a spiritual family protecting me from going too far astray, giving me what I desperately need. It's as if I never belonged to the family I was born to and I'm painfully finding my way back.

June 12, 1992. Spiritual stepping stones – paths taken and not taken.

1. Getting out of clothes that never fit me. I so desperately twisted and turned in them, trying to wear and always being pinched somewhere. Feeling lopsided, like a hem falling down behind me. My most comfortable dress was one from my cousin. Clothes were a way to hide in, trying to give the appearance of acceptability which I finally despaired of.

2. Working in the shadows of myself, driven by a passionate need to escape from what didn't suit me. Trying to justify its unsuitability.

3. Everything I did was a temporary expedient because I didn't know what else to do. I had the courage but it never seemed right. I had the means.

4. I flowered on a rock with the most meager of soil but I could make the most of it. The seed carried its own within it.

5. Now the garden is thick and overflowing where unheard of things can take root. I wait to see what will appear, naturally, of itself. The wildflowers waiting to spring, whatever forms they know to take.

17

6. Beyond the garden lives a forest. When my garden has grown, I will move on to this place and understand what it has to tell me. Instruction is unlike any other.

June 12, 1992. Intersections. The death of my mother was the beginning of my release from my sense of guilt and obligation but also my rebellion. Just the other side of the reaction to control, I felt lost without her dominating will to do battle with. Like the end of the cold war. Had she not died, I could not have proceeded with my life as I wished. I would have been stuck doing the same old dance, over and over. I could not have come to Santa Fe. I could not have disengaged from our relationship for fear it would have killed her. She had to die first.

At last, I could do what I'd been postponing, only to find myself able to do it only on the side, raising a family, as well. But my choices of what to do were different and the means were anything. There was no one looking over my shoulder. And then I began my healing work. They would never have understood, or if they had, it would have frightened them. I was free to pursue what I was finding the most meaningful, more so than as an artist in this kind of society. But this was to be impeded by my mother's representative in my life – my husband. So sick and needy he was that I felt too guilty to take care of myself.

At this point, I can choose to live my healing work authentically or to go out and get help from the most unexpected places. Small miracles that make me see.

June 12, 1992. Having understood my propensity to avoid kindly, loving people. To actually discourage any overtures. Don't get too close if you love me. I didn't know I was so frightened of genuine warmth. I didn't know that I felt any love on my part was entirely inadequate. I have slowed down enough to catch these thoughts before I bury them and so I was really undeserving. But more, I was liable to be suffocated, equating genuine love with death.

I would choose people so narcissistic they could only see me as their reflection and so entirely unavailable to me. Those that I felt safe with. But, in the end, I would be resentful and feel victimized. Giving too much to them in a grandiose gesture to compensate for my inadequacy. I was unable to recognize my needs as being truly genuine. But I passionately needed to act on them. In spite of, or perhaps a better way to say it, that I pursued it precisely because it was opposed. Because, in anger, I am well. But hardly well enough. It's like trying to fly with one wing.

All fantasy, a small child's understanding of reality. Today, I look at it, and wonder how I can reason with my irrational self that is not open to reasonable ideas. I will begin by looking at myself, today. Seeing how I leave my present. I can feel the genuine love deep down because it came with me originally, as part of the equipment. Like standing in warm sunlight, love that is just the right temperature to be growing in. I can't reason, no, I can feel the warmth of love that is there, catching it before I bury it. I can feel and keep on feeling, lowering the defenses of denial. And keep examining the battlements, stone by stone, removed with great concentration.

It's not power but values that matter. In values, there is authentic power, like the power of a seed to sprout and blossom, without reasonable words but to be alive is the thing. To value what cannot be spoken in ordinary words but what is at the bottom of all movement. Like the source of a river in a hidden place.

July 3, 1992. I must be loyal to myself and faithful to others. If I am loyal to others, I cannot be faithful. As a seeker of the truth, I need not be ashamed or even concerned with being materially poor. In my relationships, I have been more loyal to them and not to myself. I closed my eyes and reinvented reality. I am now facing reality and finding validation everywhere, in spite of a society that encourages denial. What I read and what I hear, there's enough out there, unmasking the lies because the current of truth is on the ascendance.

Not to be afraid of the pressures of money, otherwise, they have got me. That's the key. And another way is to make me feel lonely and alienated from the norm as if there were something wrong with me. I'm not buying that either. With truth as my guide, I am never alone. The whole of humanity walks with me on this journey. It's my truth but truth belongs to all of us.

July 3, 1992. Dream in the early morning. I had gone to sleep with anxieties that I knew were unreasonable. In my dream, I was my six-year-old self, pulling out all my psychic wounds and holding them up to Sensei, who was acting as the proxy of my higher self. I pulled out every one of them, like nightmarish heads made of sack-cloth and distorted. There is a parallel between my sixth year and the years I suffered from my husband, especially the years of his illness. All my psychic wounds that were pulled out included the ones I'd experienced with HKL. I held them up, each and every one of them and those that I had experienced with HKL, also. I held them up, each and every one of them so they could be counted and given recognition. Sensei was sympathizing with each one as I showed them to him. It was a purging because as they were validated, I could lay them aside and no longer have to live with them. What a blessing. I felt much happier in the morning.

Not that the purge was complete. No, not yet. There is still the loss of energy that I am experiencing. My reaction to feeling good about myself. I have to contend with those internalized, criticizing voices that wish me ill. Out of jealousy, my brother in particular. His life was impossible. But mine, perhaps more so. I had three against me and I was the littlest. I can recognize his hell but he cannot recognize mine. As a little girl, I loved him immensely but that too must be set aside. He can never validate me any more than our parents could and he is more similar to them than I am.

I feel I am more valid than my family, it is they who are the aliens. I am penetrating my journey more deeply than they and recovering my human-ness in its largest sense. I mean being autonomous, not shackled by a vaguely understood convention. Purposely vague to keep people enslaved and trying harder. People are alienated from themselves, from their truth. Honesty requires more courage to face the demons than most people are willing to cultivate. I am one of the fortunate, happy, few.

July 11, 1992. I keep feeling pain and regret because I might have made him feel rejected today. Yet the time I spend with him is precious. Whatever little he says, I'm always glad to hear, this is of primary importance. I am afraid he will feel I don't appreciate that. I go on with my life also, in my own way. I had friends to meet to go Journal writing, trying to unfold as I was meant. I feel apologetic, defensive like he was my tyrannical father. But the way is paved with misunderstandings and lack of confidence. I am the one feeling I'll be rejected if I don't give my entire life away to whoever cares about me. An extreme of sweet gratitude turned into a bitterness to poison my life. After all, he will get over it. He might even be angry with me. But I'll get over it. I think I can "control" him by sacrificing myself but that's just voodoo and I don't need to do that.

Why do I feel responsible for keeping his ego intact and at my expense? Who worries about mine? This is not the same as being discourteous. Not to abase me to keep his love, I think. Not to be abject in my love. It's not required. I can't grow that way. It's too demeaning of my spirit. What would be the use of a spiritual teacher to help me along the way? It's how I sabotage myself, it's a dirty trick. This impoverished inner child hardly believes what a beautiful soul she is. Yet knowing inside that it's true. Trying to be loyal to that one. I am feeling physical pain in my chest as if I had done some terrible crime. I'm glad to know about it. It's an absurdity, so I can expose it to the fresh air of my mind. I think about it later, there is no real separation between him and me. It's my ignorance that creates the boundary, my being impressed with him as a great being, greater than me. This impedes my progress to truth and reality. His being who he is means I can also realize myself. There. We are all equal.

Just as my enlightenment helps others, I am also these others, it goes back and forth, from me to them, and them to me, like a circle of reality. I keep seeing it as one way. Literally. But no, it's all interconnected. I am reminded of the dog next door, cringing and making herself small before my dogs. But she does it with dignity, knowing who she is as a realized dog. This gesture is a formality between them. I find I am not as realized as this dog. This dog is not afraid when she cringes. I am.

July 1, 1992. My inner child, the six-year-old, keeps grieving over all the pain from her experience of that time, wanting to die because she was no longer the treasure she had been to her family. Feeling abandoned by them because she was no longer thought worthwhile. And the bitterness and disappointment she felt in them because she knew she was very worthwhile but they were cowards and hypocrites. Having lost their faith. And how I was disloyal to myself all the time I was loyal to HKL, which could only result in illness and a broken heart. I should have listened to my six-year-old and given her comfort and reassurance. We certainly deserved better than what we got. Because I betrayed myself, I was afraid to love myself, had hoped I could save him that way. I didn't understand it was a crime against the universe. He needed to punish himself and I interfered because I needed to save him. Why?

It was not my responsibility. I was overcompensating because I didn't love myself enough. So how could I honestly have loved him if I didn't love myself? I am being loyal to myself now and to her. That poor abused little girl, who had once been a princess. She is my princess and I shall give her due respect and the love she deserves. I dreamt she was being given her due, all her wounds were being given their due recognition and sympathized with. Oh, how she was wronged. Especially the horror of what we had been through with HKL.

I woke up feeling soothed and happy with myself. Both she and I. I had gone to sleep feeling anxious but the dream resolved my feelings. Then and now. It is my darling six-year-old that I cherish which gives me ease and self-esteem. We don't need to suffer for the crimes of others. We are free to be happy and confident. There is still time in this life for simple satisfaction. Time to be open to the love of the universe within me.

We Grow by Delays

July 11, 1992 at Rauline's. I don't want to tell anyone what a rich and beautiful life I'm secretly having. The life I have always wanted and only now, widowed and alone, am able to have it. People would be envious. Outwardly, I am an object to be pitied, living from hand to mouth, which I am. But It seems I have faith enough not to feel anxious or even serious about it. I know that I am supposed to feel serious about money but that is a scam. It's such a privilege, this freedom. To live in a space I look at with delight each morning when I awaken. It's called taking care of myself, I don't have to work around someone else's needs anymore. Of course, I'm struggling, trying to face my inner blockage and overcome each hurdle as it appears without pain and struggle. I cannot grow.

I remember and old boyfriend telling me I will meet many hurdles along the way but I'll know how to climb over them as they appear. His name was Furiya, and it was our first year in art school at Cooper Union. What a loving man. But un those days I spurned warmth and love, and especially admiration. I wonder how I would feel today? Now that I'm aware of those old self-hate tendencies; I hope.

Dialogue with Ted:

Me: I grabbed you as an escape. I never suspected you were doing the same. I had trouble with reality.

Ted: I used and abused you. Hoping you would leave me so I would have an excuse for my hatred of women and drink myself to death.

Me: I took such a long time to wake up to the fact that you were gay as well as an alcoholic, and being such a hypocrite with me.

Ted: When you left me I was finally free to live the life I really wanted. It gave me a feeling of power. At last. I won.

Me: The crime was with society. That homosexuals had to hide or be ostracized. You used me as your wife to hide behind.

Ted: It was wrong of me to use you like that but I couldn't think what else to do and you were so easy to manipulate. Especially when I sent you to Italy that summer. I was hoping that you would never come back. I really couldn't stand you anymore. Especially with your success, I was so envious I preferred to look down on you so I could rationalize using you. As someone who didn't matter.

Me: I felt I didn't matter, too. That's why I let you get away with your lies and cheating. I was afraid to be alone even though being with you was a punishment.

This has been very difficult and painful for me to record. I feel ashamed of the poor creature that I was and yet, I was also doing positive things for myself. This I should remember, and with pride. It was part of the journey that I had to get through. There is no shame in that.

July 16, 1992, a dream:

Steve was standing by my door, hat in hand, very sadly wanting to apologize for lying about me and convincing Mary I was not to be believed. To apologize for his insane need to control and manipulate us. I suspect Mary made him feel threatened by her relationship with me. Maybe he was just feeling threatened by there being anyone else in her life. Even a good friend.

But it wasn't now, it was the apartment in the Bronx that I grew up in and I was at the age of a teenager. I am getting in touch with my fourteen-year-old self, desperately guilty over my mother's jealousy, not allowing me to grow into womanhood. I think I want my brother to apologize for so cruelly cutting me down with every attempt I made to grow and accomplish anything. I could not be independent. He needed to be able to manipulate me as his willing victim. I think about Steve as a comparison, he tried to cut me down because I finally created a serious piece of writing, without asking for his help or permission. He accused me of plagiarizing his work. Of being a con artist who was out to take advantage of him and Mary. The kind-hearted victims. I was busy with patients, I am always hoping for a busy practice. And I didn't have time to talk to him. He was trying to admit his mistake and apologize.

In reality, there is no chance that either of these men would acknowledge their selfishness and their unjust attitude toward me. But in my dream, I was surprised and gratified that Steve would come.

As I write this I can see this is still a painful and frustrating subject. The attitude that hurt is – once again, I am of no value as a person and can be sacrificed to their egos. Both of them need to tear me down, however cruel, feeling threatened by who I am. Strong and independent. Neither of them have enough integrity and perhaps were too afraid of me because I couldn't be controlled by them. There was a lot of pain for me in the apartment in the Bronx. It was the 1940s, I was a teenager then.

My family was like a heavy stone on my spirit. I felt angry and betrayed. How dare I become an attractive, intelligent woman? I was constantly being humiliated. I was too scared to run away so I married a monster instead. I needn't feel ashamed of my desperation. Nor should I feel ashamed about being an artist's model for a year or so. I did it to reassure myself that I was a beautiful, and sexual, woman. I was a flower trying to bloom on a rock, finding cracks and crevices to nurture me.

There is no guilt in my having rejected them. I was forced to live a secret life. I was trying to survive in spite of them. I was searching for my sanity in an insane world. Now in old age, alone and peaceful, freeing myself of false obligations, and free of the real ones as well. I am digging up the old obsessions and events, however painful. I am affirming the strength that got me through the victimization, sorting out the events and feelings. Letting my true identity emerge. I wanted to do everything. All at once.

I see how they all hang from the same thread. It only seems to spin out in time. I am doing it all now. In the moment.

July 17, 1992. There is a lot of self-hate I still have to get through. Not to depend on outside approval, especially in a poor economy with an unfair tax structure. A society where women still feel jealous of other women – I hope this is not true of all women. I ask, why are all the great nations suddenly so poor since Russia broke up? Is this the beginning of this society breaking up? Hopefully, this government will change and things will improve. National healthcare should include what I do.

The morning after a rain, after a dry spell, what a lovely thing to wake up to. And yet, I have to keep reassuring myself I'm on the right track and worthy to be on it. Sometimes I still react to my awakenings with a counter-negative, some insane voice threatening me. Not my voice. I find that I am suddenly being incapable of what I normally do because my self is emerging from all the trash. Rising out of all the debris, I don't have to be a ruin.

DIALOGUE WITH TIME

Time: I am an illusion. What can you understand?

Me: I am timeless but I don't understand.

Time: I am a god that you created to divide space with.

Me: In this limited body, I can only see one piece at a time.

Time: It is all timeless, undivided. Get beyond the body's limits.

Me: Deep into the well of my being, I keep reemerging, as each body fades.

Time: You are always the same person, searching and going beyond the limits of a programmed barrier.

Me: Always barriers created by the program but I am more than my computer self. With each life, I discover the same thing, and climb over the same barriers.

Time: Mirrors and projections, all are yours. The barriers exist only within your own field. The system is limited to only a small measure of yourself. Find the system-less system.

Me: What gives me a life system? Unlike any system I know, it is ever changing and unraveling its mystery to me.

Time: Don't give credence to illusions. Be firm in your confidence. Keep coming back to that firm inner center when you fall back into the programmed illusions.

Me: To forgive myself, keeps the gate open. A fortress is only as strong as its shut gates. The fortress is crumbling of itself because a gate remains open.

Time: Time and space don't exist. A fortress crumbles because you only thought it existed. It was created sitting on your mother's lap and from the back of your father's head. And the brother who could only see his reflection rendering you invisible.

Me: My invisibility, my real existence denied, I keep retreating under the table. A false security, I will find myself out.

Time: In the shadows they said, 'Who do you think you are to escape our grasp?' But that time is only an image on a screen. Unlike now, which pulsates with reality.

Me: What reality do I see here? Not a physical one, with the illusion of time and space, unravelling – unwinding itself. I'm contacting the light behind the film projection, that irrational aliveness that rules me. That following is my only hope for this cycle.

Time: See you next..

July 22, 1992. Now I am starting to see it. Why Sensei would never answer my questions about the medical work, and not let me treat patients in Mexico when he let everyone else. He had a selfish dependency on me that is how he loves and was afraid of losing me if I became too proficient and confident. I would be less dependent on him. He never thought about what would be of benefit to me or about all the pain he caused me by his abuse. He is a great and courageous man but on a personal level, he is too neurotic. I attract brilliant men into my life but always too dependent on me and need to keep me under their control. I am glad Sensei didn't try to keep me in Santa Fe when I told him that I wanted to go to Seattle. That would have been too hard for me and I might have stayed, however reluctantly. He would have felt obligated to me, and that he was too proud to do. It would have lowered his position with me.

I hope I can get my own act together and not need to repeat the miserable relationship I had when my parents were alive, over and over again. Going nowhere.

I think in my first years of life I was truly cherished by my mother. She told me she had dreamt, when she was pregnant with me, that she saw a big boat coming over the ocean and when it approached, she could see her mother's name on it, in big letters. This was the mother who died when my mother was nine years old. She never stopped grieving for her. I was her mother coming back to her. So I was cherished for all the wrong reasons and to the detriment of my older brother's self-esteem. I think that is why they were trashing me. I am still a kind and caring person, the way it's natural for a human being to feel towards others. I really had a miserable life with them. It seems in those experiences in my early years helped me to keep my sanity and strong will to do right by myself.

So perhaps with this step 4 meeting that I just joined I can clear out my false self and get to the truth. It hit me so powerfully around the issue of asking my needs to be met. Maybe I will be able to relate to people who aren't so needy and will be kind to me. Perhaps I have learned that I won't need them to be so needy for my security. If they are so much in need of me they will resent it and have to dominate me to maintain their sense of independence. I shouldn't be afraid to be friends with people who don't need me. Maybe it's too much to hope that a kind and loving person will turn me on the way my fantasy persons did. It may be past my time for that. But at least get out of my isolation and have real friends who won't begrudge me my recovery. That would be the ultimate healing.

July 29, 1992. Remembering as a teenager how I wanted to hide my sexually maturing body, ashamed to have anyone see me. Don't look at me! Why was something so natural, even joyful, a source of shame? What did it mean to my family? I was becoming an independent self with my own power. My mother was envious and has separation anxiety. My father was afraid of his love for me so he became rude and insulting. I was never good enough. My brother was jealous because he was ugly and afraid for himself. They all needed me to remain their victim and I might be able to walk away. I was breaking the intricately woven web of our relationships. The denial and manipulations keep me in my place.

I want to cherish who I was then and who I am now. Even now I am afraid to stand up for myself for fear of being cut down. My mind goes blank when I need to answer someone's slight. Only years later do I think of a good answer. I bow down as a victim just to keep my head. It's only a role I play compulsively for fear of losing my head. I'm trying to recover the knowing part of me I've suppressed. All those times HKL made me so angry and miserable. I had to walk out of the house or wound up crying on the couch because I couldn't stand to remain in bed with him. For a brief moment, I could stop loving him and feel independent but I was afraid to break up the marriage. I was afraid he would abandon me and our small children. I hadn't the courage without any other means of support, emotionally or financially. I understand now that to love someone meant my giving up who I was. I didn't know any other way.

I am finding compassion for myself and forgiveness. It's the way toward self-love. I'm peeling away the layers of the false self that I built up for what I at one time needed to survive. As a child, I'm searching for the courage to get beyond my fear of being undone. I need to cherish the compliments to my self-esteem like when Doris said I'm a blessing – I need to know that.

July 30, 1992. It's been so difficult for me to finally see how my father engaged in emotional incest with me but now it makes sense. My feelings and his, he had to distance himself physically, even when I was a baby. I never knew his touch or any kind of affection. No wonder I was always cuddling my uncle when he visited. I was so starved to be hugged and held. He simply couldn't be a normal human father. As I became sexually mature, he could only be verbally abusive, the attention could only be negative. Which accounts for a lot of my mother's jealousy and her derogatory attitude towards me. It was competition for her. I suspect she emotionally engaged in incest with my brother the same way. They were so childish and insecure. They were overwhelmed by children who outdistanced them in education and ability to be part of this society that for them was so foreign and frightening.

They were terribly proud of us but at the same time alienated. They grew afraid we'd look down on them. My mother pretended I was stupid and ugly and once remarked that this educated woman she admired was so kind to be my friend. Or when she bought me a pair of scissors and showed me how to cut out material for my maternity clothes. She said I should be creative, ignoring the fact I was already a professional artist. Now I feel sad for them and appreciative of what it must have been like for them to struggle against so many odds. Still, having grown up in a family where I was constantly criticized, denied what I needed. It's hard for me to love myself or let others love me. I create an unreal relationship, expecting to be hurt and belittled, afraid of getting emotional support because I don't trust it.

I want to change my behavior, my vibration so that I don't numb out when I'm being criticized. Sensei does have his insane moments, which I can expect from time to time. But I don't have to play into his hands, either. I need to remember, he's different from my father. He has his own insanity and I don't have to retreat into a child's dependence and fear.

July 31, 1992. I'm so scared when men might like me. If they are friendly or even just polite. I'm afraid they want something from me, make demands. I exaggerate their interest in me, ignoring the fact that I am an old woman now. Why does it scare me? I can own my power. I know how to set boundaries, I'm not helpless. As if what they need is what I'm compelled to give without an opinion of my own that is valid. I blank out as if I don't know anything and must follow their lead. Whatever they tell me I must follow without question. But I can love them on whatever level, without giving myself away to them. That's my fear, to abandon myself. I feel their neediness and it makes me afraid. Or I expect them to be needy and I'm afraid I'll let them drink my blood. Especially with men.

My hope is to overcome this paralysis and free myself, to love myself strongly enough so I don't have to be afraid I'll give way. I can feel confident in my own power that I can handle whatever real situation comes up. I keep obsessing about Sensei's attacking me and humiliating me in front of other students. Why does he make it so difficult for me? The others look down on me, also, following his lead. How do I answer him? What do I do? It's only a matter of time before he pulls it on me again. I feel I'm being victimized by someone who actually loves me a great deal. I ask myself, am I so sure that he does? Perhaps if I remember to love myself at that moment. Not to take his cruel words seriously as if he were right. Not to take on the victim role that I automatically fall into. Maybe that's the test: to be sure of me and not of be afraid of rejection. To depend only on myself and my unique destiny.

If only I could rise up to it. He has such impossibly high standards that mostly he's disappointed with himself for not having been able to achieve more. These expectations make him so impossible at times. I may have a solution. When he's abusive, to look him straight in the eye, from my void place, and see what happens. It will be terrifying for me but I must do it.

August 3, 1992. My cousin called suggesting we have a reunion with our brothers at the wedding my brother is making for his son in October. I said I wasn't invited and since he never returned my call when my husband died, I didn't expect an invitation either. I added that my childhood memories were too painful to want to be re-lived that way. I think she was a little shocked at my truthfulness as well as disappointed. She always said her life was boring. Even now. I suppose a reunion appeals to her as a little less than boring. A terrible pall came over me after I hung up. I was again that abused, and hurt child feeling she wasn't worth anything, and being manipulated. Her healthy rebellion was unacceptable. I momentarily forgot the person I actually am.

And then I got in touch with my source of wisdom and reality. There is no way I should go and be put into the pit again. They are all alien to me and it would be meaningless to spend time with them again, without any hope of affirmation. I realized that my sentimentality was vacillating. However, this conclusion came as a great relief and the pall lifted. I was back in the present although there is still a remainder of a small knot of grief in my heart. If my brother does send an invitation, I will make my excuses and just say I'm much too busy. Chances are he won't, and it's just as well. I have to stop holding onto the dream of who I would like him to be and accept the person he really is. I tend to recreate everybody in my own image, which is absurd. I go on with my recovery, shedding the old baggage, piece by piece.

Peaks, Depths and Explorations

August 8, 1992. So many things running through my head. Snatches of conversation with this one and that. Feeling cheerier because of the bit of socializing these last few days. It does muddle my head and makes it hard to stay in focus. I've been thinking about moving to Seattle where Joe and his family live. I've been feeling so hemmed in here and isolated. I wanted to break out. It's in abeyance until October. But in the meantime, I'm acting as if I will and I'm starting to unload things like the Taos bed, where HKL and I used to sleep, and where he slept alone towards the end where I left him with his catheter.

It would never have occurred to me to get rid of it except in this context and of course, it has lost its usefulness in my life and it's time to let the charming hulk go. In fact, the idea of leaving Santa Fe lit a fire under me and I'm starting to expand more. I have to learn how to balance my solitariness with some friends so I don't get stuck. Going out there was surprisingly scary for fear of rejection. I must still be sick – it's so unlike me.

I must be careful not to get that way, or maybe it's because I'm just coming out of a drought and the healing is happening as time passes. I need distance from this period of many changes in order to see this process from a different perspective. I'm digging in and working on the program and I don't want too many distractions. It's too easy to avoid the inner work, to catch those fleeting moments of insight before I retreat in denial.

My present situation is so beautifully conducive to doing what I have kept postponing in the past. There are some days of depression where I have no will to use my time well. That's when I imagined changing it all. The thought of traveling 1,650 miles to Seattle and beginning again is both terrifying and exciting. I have put the thought out there and we'll see what comes back. I'd really like to have more patients to treat, it seems such a waste.

August 9, 1992. The themes running through my life. Peaks, depths, and explorations; the process of searching. One doesn't know where one is going, the event has its own timing. Don't push for closure, just search. The meaning of my life is like an acorn that hasn't started yet. It isn't there yet. Connect this with roads not taken, some things that haven't had a chance to live. Use twilight imagery, let moments come, look at them later. Let images flow. Imagery extension, what does the image lead to?

Yearning to breathe free, feeling a tightness in my chest when I say that. Grief and fear, my resistance to allowing myself to be free. Each morning, I ask that my self-hate be removed from me and I experience waves of love and understanding envelop me. Grief and remorse, wishing I could have done it all better. And then seeing how the experience and events all led me to who and where I am now. All purposeful, and running along one thread. I cannot fall into self-denial again, where I compulsively give myself away. There is an obligation to let my own flower emerge, it's so easy to lose energy when it's for myself. At those times I don't fight it, better to let it pass, trusting my inner will to pull me out of it and perhaps discover what it behind it.

I remember the faces of my friends at various times here, with the backdrop of the mountains at twilight. How we came here to begin again. The climb up by a different route. How hard we worked to follow the new way of thought, willing to work at anything just to remain here. How few of us remained. How it transformed us. Some of us lost their mind. I am still here but I may soon be making a closure on the last twenty years, as another is attempting to emerge. I'm here with the background of the mountains at twilight. Today there was a magnificent rainbow with the setting sun. At the peak of the mountain. It seemed to be bidding me a fond farewell, telling me I will be fortunate in my next move away.

I keep wondering if I should stay, is there still ground to dig here, unearthing more treasures that would change me further? Is this really the time to take my journey to another place where I hopefully can be more actively engaged? I wonder if I am leaving it all behind again when it really needs ripening. A different vision to apply to it. There is a nervous restlessness, something must change, and perhaps waiting will show me the way. My feelings of impatience may be coming from my resistance to new things coming. But need it to be here, in Santa Fe? I am learning to trust more. Perhaps, staunchly holding onto my place here, things are starting to gather around me. The process is so slow but maybe surer than trying to create it with brilliant plans and strategies that finally fall to nothing. Leaving us wasted like the school that we had built with our hands. So many hours I spent running it for him and writing the books with him. It all turned sour and perverse, contrary to its original intention.

Let it happen to itself, just be there to catch it and to help light the way. Well, if I can read the signs, I'll let the indications guide me. No more plans but needing to act as well as be quiet, I will be alert to it. I do not want to wait too long either. I need to move and to break free, inside and outside. To regain the lost ground when I set myself aside for a higher purpose. It's time to reintegrate and clarify my issues and resistances. To get at my devils that cannot stand the light. When he said that Sharon would have to move out of New Mexico to practice, where he decides to send her. I felt like I was taking up someone else's space here. Typical of my self-negation and caving into his harshness. Ignoring his love and need of me. I need to be needed too much. Let outside events speak to me now.

I called Joe and he said he would do everything that he could to help me if I would come. My darling boy. Both he and his wife have opened their arms out to me.

Stepping Stones 9/17/1992.

- Mama's darling, she is ignoring my older brother, abandoning him to over-indulge me.
- Getting off mama's lap one day, at age three, declaring my independence of her smothering self-indulgence. The war never ended until she died.
- My brother never forgave me for being so bright and cute. Needing to me to be his creature, insisting I was ugly and stupid and couldn't succeed at anything except by mistake.
- Fortunes changed. In our poverty, I became everybody's victim. I remember still a dream from that time my family turned into vicious snakes, attacking me cruelly. I was so frightened but it was true.

- Learning to stand alone but not free to the self-hate and guilt that was fostered. I would be nobody's creature. No matter what the price. Even alienation.
- Feeling alienated. Not worthwhile. And very angry at the injustice.

My brother was a newspaper delivery boy, he promised to pay me for taking his route one day, to help him. I did but he never paid me. I felt betrayed. I had wanted to see "The Wizard of OZ" so badly. I needed 10 cents and I finally found the means by taking in glass milk deposit bottles and saving the pennies. I walked a mile to the movie house but it was 11 cents – a penny tax. And they wouldn't let me in. I can still see the ticket seller's unyielding face. My brother would not give me the penny.

But it was still playing the following week and over-joyed at getting another chance, I managed the 11 cents. The movie was heavenly. I was not disappointed at all. I was overwhelmed by the magic and the satisfaction. There's another world out there where I can be triumphant, happy, and accepted.

9/17/1992, at Penny's house. Getting out of the hole I've been sitting in, going to try my wings in Seattle. All is changing. I'm shaking off the dust from my feet. All that passed, the misery, and the teaching, and the awakening it became. No use hanging on to a mode that no longer serves. Now to put it all into practice. To continue the journey where I feel the fruit was meant to fall. The fulfillment of an age of preparation. Leaving behind the role I've outgrown. That time has caused to wither. An old, moldy skin was discarded. Yes. There's nostalgia and love for this place and there will always be a relationship that will continue but in another form. I'm trusting this decision is correct and that Seattle will be successful for me. That the blockage will fall away and I can freely do my work. As I said to Sensei, I have no hope here in Santa Fe, so it's time to move on. To start my life anew. HKL's dying left me free.

The next step can't happen yet. Going deeper. To feel the patient's diagnosis from a distance. To watch over David. Without saying so. I find that I am still blocking myself. Like standing on the edge, unable to go forward. Perhaps this will change even before I leave. I was talking to David K and he was telling me how he does it. Treating from afar. Writing this is how I decided to tell my friends here about my decision, the one I was pondering last month with them.

9/17/1992, Inner dialogue.

little me: I felt so angry at the abuses and unkindness of older people. They don't know or understand me. Didn't know they should love me. It was hard to love myself but I was doggedly determined to get what I needed, somehow. Yet, there was a boundary I didn't dare step over. It would have been frightening.

Big Me: Today I know I'm capable of walking over that boundary but I don't dare because it would make me very happy and somehow that means total abandonment. So I'm still afraid despite that I'm standing alone now and my life has been vastly improved for it.

little me: There is just so much I can fight off by myself without some outside reinforcements to encourage me on. But I avoid being loved and nurtured because it means being drowned in it. I would be like re-entering the womb, I must reject my mother's embrace if I'm to live.

Big Me: I still have difficulty recognizing the love others have for me but now that I am leaving, how it all comes into focus. Yes, I need others to be dependent on me to feel trustful of them. I can see it's not just that. There has been love and kindness all along. Not just on my side. They wish me well in spite of their losing me. They can manage and be alright. Mom always made me feel she would actually die if I left her. I couldn't strike out on my own really. Like Dorothy in the Wizard of Oz, I couldn't strike out on the path of the Wizard, until she did die.

little me: We are free now, both of us, I put my hands into yours. I got stuck somewhere along the way. Remaining in a haunted circle. Now we can get out together. I give you my passionate longing and optimism for succeeding.

Big Me: We're stepping out of the circle's spell. Speaking the words necessary, the free incantation. I finally learned it. I'm peeling away the crusty, old, skin along the road. Stepping along with the child's original skin again. Young and fresh and unintimidated. Another chance, a continuation, unhindered. Along the yellow-brick road.

September 17, 1992.   Twilight Imagery.   Green trees going down a hill, a moist blue sky, a wide-open road like a deserted highway. We are hand-in-hand in anticipation approaching a meadow leading into a valley. On the other side of the mountains, the descent makes walking easy. We have come down from the mountain. We didn't know this place we are entering but it feels right and welcoming and so kind and reasonable about our reality. Our reality was denied for so very long. The truth of me.

Even last week, the old nightmare was being played again. My brother was so angry when I said I was still grieving and didn't want to go to his son's wedding. He said, in effect, that my feelings were not real and got angry and hung up on me when I stood my ground. If he is angry, so what?? What difference does it make? Where has he been all these years, anyway? The big wedding he is making is for his own ego gratification, assuming a patriarchal position. But he is too stingy with the "largesse." The hypocrite. He was being thwarted by my reality. But it makes no difference to me whatever he does. But I relived the old scene where I felt I had to apologize for myself. That I wasn't worthwhile. And I felt so great when I could say no and not be afraid of the consequences. I could see him for the selfish person that he really is, not the persistent idealization of him that I had loved.

There is nothing to lose but my illusions. I am real. I have declared it. And so is my vision of reality. Now to continue the work of unraveling and discarding. The work of emergence. Happiness is allowed and reasonable. Feeling good to read all of this to my friends. Explaining it all to me and to them as well. They responded with warmth and encouragement, saying how they will miss me.

October 12, 1992. Just because I feel sad and vulnerable today doesn't mean I have to look down on myself as being inferior and shameful. I will be as kind and gentle with myself. Loving myself as a worthwhile person. I am still that capable, powerful woman I was yesterday.   I am just feeling scared because the time is drawing closer to departure and there is a part of myself that doesn't think I deserve happiness and success. I will just sit with those negative thoughts and bathe them with love and understanding, like a good parent to that scared inner child. It's ok to be feeling that way right now.

Spiritual Stepping Stones to Seattle

November 21, 1992. Journal writing group meeting at my house. A house emptied of furniture and memories. Twenty years of it. I haven't wanted to seriously look at it. It was too hard. I was just putting one foot in front of the other to get the job done. Letting go of the past, one item at a time. I leave in two weeks and it is time to write about it.

I keep remembering incidents with my husband. How long ago when he was still well, when we did this and when we got that. Remembering my son's growing up here. Remembering with pleasure my astonishment at how brilliant and insightful they were turning out to be. My style of kids! I was grateful for it, feeling fortunate with them. And the years of misery with him, particularly as his illness worsened both of us losing our minds over it. I realize now I should never have remodeled to make an office at home. My patient load never recovered from that hiatus. Better to have opened an office elsewhere and not have remained stuck and isolated with him and all the negative energy in the house. But I could never have "abandoned" him; I kept hoping I could somehow "save" him. An operation, perhaps? How little did I know that his heavy guilt feelings could never be healed? It would have been a disaster in one form or another. He couldn't permit happiness for him or me. Our fatal marriage – never again!

I'm glad I re-did the bedroom where most of the illness went on. And the bathroom. A necessary purification. Well, he is in a better place now and I am recovering from those years of torture I allowed him to inflict on me. I am taking back my life. Free to just be me.

Sometimes I'm scared to leave, now that the reality of it is approaching. What am I doing? Am I really doing this? So I get into a better space in my head and say, why not? Why not indeed! I must say goodbye to this house with all its ghosts, respectfully, thankfully, that has enriched my life and helped me to grow into the person I am now. The person I have yet to fully discover, so different from how I grew up, as the child of immigrants. Uneducated, ambitious but superstitious, and fearful of this new society whose language they don't know. Some of it rubbed off on me, I still see in my brother and cousins, limiting their minds against radically different approaches to life.

February 11, 1993. Here in Seattle, I realize how I escaped with my life and I am still in recovery, evolving into quite another person. I am thinking of letting go of that early life, of no longer contacting old family, now that I am here, it seems meaningless anymore.

It's up and down, so it's clear to see that when I'm down, I am mad at Sensei for all the miserable, humiliating, unfair things he's pulled in me. And when I'm up, I love him and feel so grateful that he had come into my life and done so much for me. He is both a monster and a redeemer and I have to accept him for all his qualities, good and bad. That's who he is, all of it. Perhaps this is what I need in order to grow, and that nothing is a mistake. I hate playing his game even though I know I could get more from him if I did. More rewards. But he invites hypocrisy. The men and women of the world who know how to pay him, to use him for their own selfish ends. But most of the world is selfish and maybe he understands and accepts that. Perhaps he thinks that they won't do anything for him unless it is also in their interest to do so.

Sensei distrusts everyone and suspects my idealism. He can't believe that I understand what to do for him, and the work of the Kototama is also in my own best interests because I cannot stand the world the way it is, and at least Kototama offers hope for a better future. He can't believe that my innate kindness and good heart are what make me happy. That is what is in it for me.

Too bad he is such a poor judge of character, he once told me that he knew that about himself. So I must go my way as best I can, accepting the reality of what is and trying not to expect anything. To sit back and trust that whatever comes is what I need for my further growth and understanding. It's no use to feel angry and indignant about the lack of fairness, that is also necessary and ultimately there is no difference between good and bad. Both sides contribute to the furtherance of humanity.

I was thinking about the tenant, Yula, whom I had to forcibly remove from the house so I could move in. She had a good game going, living rent-free because of Joe's kindness and sympathy. He hated to chance to be in the wrong. I had to pull out my "sword." He said that he couldn't have done what I did and it took my insistence and clarity to see what she was up to. As he said, to put my foot down. I think he would have had to, sooner or later, as time dragged on and she tried to keep it up for as long as possible. She was furious with me that she couldn't win more free time than she did. I saw right through her game. But she was necessary to teach both Joe and me even though she took the negative role. All humanity is in this together, until the end of time, when we receive full consciousness.

The worst and the best are all part of the plan. Not to be proud or self-hating. Rather be grateful for whatever shards of light are reflected in our awareness. Perhaps to see the light itself when it's possible to recognize indirectly. I am feeling closer to awakening my understanding of the Kototama sounds, slowly as each layer peels away from my mind. All this suffering and joy as well. That I didn't stop and die in Santa Fe, has contributed to this present stage. That's what I want more than anything. To be alive to the sounds, what they mean, to finally see the truth. And I am thinking I can accept my own shortcomings. That I can get to what's important. When I see my Sensei's imperfections, it gives me courage and confidence.

February 23, 1993. It gets pretty discouraging when I see all the ignorance around me and nobody questioning. Everyone is so brainwashed in materialism and a robot mentality. They are all puppets, unaware of all the strings. How do I help them find their real mind? Perhaps I need to have stronger confidence in myself and not get upset when confronted with it. I'm not quick enough with the right response, automatically, my first reaction is to doubt myself and accept what is said as the authority. Then I can't think clearly and only much later do I realize it is insanity, theirs and mine. That is how people become enslaved. By doubting what they know to be the truth and afraid to argue with what is clearly blind and stupid. It is more acceptable than the truth.

Joe has a quick mind and is relatively free from being intimidated. He can always think of a good answer. His mind doesn't trip over the "shoulds" and "should nots." My intelligence has to be freed from the old intimidations, not just of my childhood but also from present society's wrong assumptions. I am fighting for my real life while the robot society remains in control. I must overcome the deadly pal that's been laid on everyone's mind, symbolized as Noah's flood. I want to be able to answer people who are filled with fear and who cover it over with arrogance. If I can give them a feeling of security and self-love, it would melt their defenses and release their clear thinking. I must totally release myself, first. Getting more synchronized with the sounds is ultimately the only way. Patients will come and students, too. So I can tell them about it.

May 19, 1993. Spiritual Stepping Stones.

1. I'm in a dark tunnel, trying to crawl out.

2. It's pre-dawn. I'm walking in a meadow, grayness waiting for the light.

3. Morning. I'm in Seattle. Really here. In this place.

4. Only a stone should be left alone.

5. In the dawn of my new life, I am looking for friends. Those with experience of the journey.

6. I'm caged in this office. So few come to visit. But when they come, I give them my light. I must wait for them.

7. I obsessed on Sensei to fill the gaping wound in my belly. I have returned to very early childhood and come back out again to here. I am whole, as I once was. The crooked life in between has shifted to somewhere else, taking the wound with it.

8. I am in a vineyard, eating ripe, black grapes.

9. The sun is hot but I am in the shade.

10. There are trees lining the path where young men are waiting. I walk past them to the tree at the end of the path, unoccupied, waiting for me. I must let go of the innocent as well.

11. An old black woman in a long dress and head scarf is approaching me, out of the vineyard, smiling.

12. She is my darkness shining with light, the one that knows, has always known, and is confident. At first, I hesitate to even acknowledge her but now I embrace her. Feeling happiness and gratitude for my lucky escape.

January 16, 1993. Twilight imagery. Still trying to settle in here. I see a golden plain. I'm walking almost vertically uphill, like a staircase. Step by step, I'm not entirely present, my head isn't totally here. I'm trying to make this place my own. So I can reach the top step, where I can see out over the valley. Across the lake to the mountains, so friendly these mountains. They welcome me. It takes psychic time to heal the rift of departure from the old and familiar. To quell the fears of change and the unknown, to reaffirm my faith in the rightness of my decision. What is out there is giving me reassurance. Like the strange way, we got the house. The duplex that would settle both me and Joe, in order to do our respective work. Marcelle doesn't have the awareness yet to realize how she needs this place, too.

So I am feeling grateful that the way is being shown to me. Here in this little office where I am putting out a healing vibration so that patients will come here. I'm also putting out ads, to show them where to come. But they will find their way, those who are searching their way. The valley is dark now with the lights of the city just coming on. The mountains are fading in the misty night. There is still light where I stand. Can the light from within me light the way for those in the city? Dispelling their ignorance, soothing their grief? I have been shown and I need to show it to them, those who are asking. I walk back to my office where the light shines like a beacon. My practice is to stay in the right space that higher dimension of knowing, despite my present circumstances and my present limitations. I must expand my light to the marketplace as best I can.

January 24. Dream. Last week I had a dream. I was driving a VW bus, a dark brilliant blue. It had to do with HKL and I, his getting me into a false situation at a ranch-style house where people were living that we were visiting. The people there were full of pretensions to spirituality and truth, but in reality, they were really in the dark. They reminded me of the place near Nambe, NM where I read my poetry and received much recognition from the people there who were following some healer from India and were trying to recruit more members, like me. He didn't want me to offend them by speaking my mind. This is somehow related to the house we were buying right now and our concern in getting Yula, the present tenant, to move out without any more fuss. She hasn't been paying the rent and wants to see what money she can get out of Joe for moving. It's a mentality that thinks it can survive only by manipulation and power plays.

Then I was driving the car myself. The landscape is still Santa Fe but HKL is already dead. I take the wrong turn and wind up on the edge of a cliff. The only one who can help me save the car (save the dream) is Joe, who comes, very annoyed at being asked. He came with his friends, Aaron, Derrin, Matt and they do it. His annoyance is like when I got him to help me set up the office in Seattle, but he does it anyway. The dream reminded me that had I stayed on in Santa Fe, my life, my dream – would have been destroyed. I shudder to think what would have become of me if I didn't have the courage, and the pain, to drive me out of a dangerous situation, psychically dangerous. It was something HKL had gotten me into but which I had passively followed.

I'm leading the way for myself now and something inside is changing, I can see it in my face and in the way my hair looks. Finding my authentic self at last. I am grateful to Joe, and to his young friends for their spirit and innocence. I am grateful to them for being my allies. I think about Marcelle, who isn't at all sure how she feels about me. I have to let her find out for herself. It's not something intellectual but her gut feelings of unsureness and suspicion. Maybe she will see I'm not a threat but a blessing.

And I am realizing how I have gotten into the rhythm of the rain, here in Seattle, even the recent hurricane we had, I feel akin to the wetness here as opposed to the desert I came out of. The hurricane reminded me of one we had in the Bronx when I was a child. I compared Seattle to the wetness of New York, another coastal city. Although New York is impossible to live in anymore. I think it was after that experience that I felt melted into the environment of Seattle. Like I have always been here. I like the rain.

November 21, 1992, typed March 3, 1993. Twilight Imagery. Walking along the beach, looking at the moonlight, I am an adolescent out of step with everyone else. I look at the moon and feel comforted, where things are free of constraints and pressure to be molded into someone I was not. I could speak better to the trees, the mountains the landscape somehow was a comfort to me.

Approaching New York City, leaving my Penna home behind. I remember the last breakfast on the porch with the falling leaves around me and the New York City scene where I was so stimulated intellectually and as an artist. But I decided it was no place to raise a family, although the children loved New York. But my husband and I were pulling apart, we were each on our own ego-trip. There were so many of them.

The magnificent mountains again. Reliving my childhood longing for natural surroundings, the blue snow on winter nights, trying to stay warm with a wood-burning stove. I remember the walk home at night [in Upstate New York] with heavy snow falling, abandoning the overloaded car at the bottom of the hill. It was overloaded with foodstuffs bought in New York for my health food store in Margaretville. And then seeing Santa Fe for the first time as a visitor. It was after a drought, everything was very dry and dusty. I remember feeling so inspired by such a strange place. This is really a place of transition in my life, I realize it now, to learn and to change, to do things that I never expected to be doing. It was like a crucible, losing the old, false identity and opening to what was really underneath. I remember my son's wedding at Orchets Island near Seattle, a taste of unspoiled wilderness. My work will be there. Perhaps I'm really a nomad, wandering from lesson to lesson. I belong to no place and to all places on earth.

March 23, 1993. I feel like I'm falling into little pieces. This waiting for patients so I can make some kind of living again. I came here so I could do better. I know I will but I will be glad when it happens. But even more deeply, I am slowly entering the sounds more. This is what really matters, above all else. And it gives me great joy, with each inch, as I get closer. Now I feel sick with panic, a feeling of weakness in my guts. I want to hide in a corner, roll up into a ball. It is hard to accept this great gift from the universe. This great love. May my self-hate be removed from me, those nagging criticisms of who do you think you are. I cannot be loved unless I'm dark and miserable – unlovable.

So much of this negative onslaught came from my brother, a child's primitive brutality and resentment that I had been born. That I could be of any value to anyone. What a miserable, hurt little boy he was and his little sister was the recipient of his rage and frustration into adulthood. Even now. Each time I unlock my office door, I hear his voice saying how can a stupid jerk like you think she can be taken seriously, as a professional. You have an office but you can't even unlock the door. When I came to Seattle to begin a new life I freed myself from him and the rest of the family, everyone, ghosts and all. But I have to recognize what is still clinging to me, the remnants and accept that some of it I still carry. I ignore it at my peril, it is my recognition to honor the pain and the sorrow that still haunt me. Only then can I reintegrate all the little pieces of myself. I had torn myself apart with self-hate so that he would not hate me. When I think of that child, so filled with love and adoration for her older brother, hating myself because he hated me, I could never do right.

find their way, those who are searching their way.

The valley is dark now, with the lights of the city just coming on. The mountains are fading in the mist of night. There is still light where I stand. Can the light from within me light the way for those in the city, dispelling their ignorance, soothing their grief? I have been shown and I need to show to them, those who are asking.

I walk back to my office, where the light shines, like a beacon. My practice is to stay in the right space, that higher dimension of knowing, despite my present circumstance and my present limitations; to expand my light to the marketplace as best I can.

As I honor that little girl today, the pain leaves me, the panic of the "Sky is Falling Chicken Little." I return to the present, a future and happy life doing just what she always wanted to do at last. I don't have to be afraid. I love her.

April 18, 1993. Dream. I don't actually remember much of the dream itself but it was so rich in imagery and resolution of problems long dormant. It left me a feeling of good even now. I'm recreating myself based on a mold that only now is being used. I have three molds, the one of daughter and the one of wife, and now, the one of a mature woman (wise crone) which is still emerging from the labyrinth. There were many rooms in the apartment but a lot of it took place in my little bedroom. My first dog Bucky was there and other people and hallways. It was there, maybe at age 8, that the molds were being formed as possibilities. This last mold is confident and whole. Made at a time when I knew what I knew naturally and wasn't yet scared into playing a role in order to please whoever I felt dependent on. Not yet aware of society's pressures to toe the line lest I be guilty.

In the dream there was a sense of clarity and pristine light, a generosity of space that couldn't have been physical space, maybe it was the room I needed to maneuver in my head. It was before I started making people up to fit my needs and ideals, ignoring their reality. I'm beginning to see people as they are now, like a heavy veil is being lifted, accepting and not being judgmental about it. They just are, and that's where I need to begin with wherever we are at the present. Not adhering to rigid rules I am slowly shedding like old clothes that never fit right, I am getting to my reality. The roles, of course, were real but were not a direct expression of my core self. As I am free to be the self I love, I don't have to hate others for not being confined to my rigid boundaries. I find myself saying, so what and why not?

And my beloved son, Joe who doesn't impose himself, what he may think of his mother should be like? We are mutually a resource and supportive to each other on so many levels. And he's remaining true to himself. To thine own self be true, words I should have said to those faculty wives in Columbus, Ohio thirty years ago. They were being conned into becoming dull housewives, sacrificing their needs and hopes, sublimating them for husbands and family. I was a terrible threat to their house of cards, by my example. And where are they now, I wonder. Probably old and discarded for a more interesting prospect and younger. They had made themselves so dull and compliant.

It took me thirty years to think about what to say to them. I, too, was caught up in looking up to the men as the authority, however selfish and tyrannical. I was also enslaved by society's edict that self-seeking women were selfish and punishable by self-loathing that I didn't buy into it so wholeheartedly. The men, I notice, are so emotionally dependent on their women, vulnerable, which is the hook that loving women get caught on. I think the confident, independent self is also based on my mother as a role model. The part of himself she loved but had to abandon after a nervous breakdown. Her healthy self, intelligent and fun-loving that she passed on to me as well as the sick role models dictated by the convention that she had to cave into.

In the myth, Ariadne shows him the way out of it, the center of the labyrinth holding the Minotaur, the animal self, materialism, and destruction. He must descend into it first, to discover it but she shows him the way out again. I see it as the course humanity has taken, those characteristics relegated to the feminine self, kept submerged as and thought of as no vale, and outside of the doings of "men" is what will bring us back to being completely human again. The killing of the robot self will be guided by the higher judgment self. We can be free, like a ship unshackled from its moorings, allowed to float freely on the ocean again. O-Harai Norito. This is what I am attempting to do. To be an example for others to follow. It is much bigger than my personal life, it's part of the wave of the reintegration of humanity.

"Right," In This Society Always Means "Wrong"

January 24, 1993. David's finally in a decent job, working for Munson Gallery, continuing the framing work he had been doing for Plaza Poster Gallery. His exacting, patient work is finally been given its due. Plaza Posters will be giving their work to Munson to do and they sold them all their equipment so they will still have Dave doing the picture framing for them. And it seems He will be paid a decent wage, with health insurance. I'm really proud and relieved it's finally going his way. I'm sure this will boost his creative ideas as well. For his own work, there is nothing more stimulating than a little soul-balm to get the ideas to flow. And Joe is on a plateau right now. It's all changing around him and he doesn't know how to go. He is going to figure it out for himself and it will be the next step forward in his development. I'm rooting from the sidelines, watching with great interest how things work out for them in keeping faith with their inner integrity. That's what I'm really proud of after all.

I am waiting to settle into my own space, to see where I can go in my inner understanding and growth. I need a quiet corner where I can make sounds, undisturbed in my concentration. I am doing what I can at the office but I'll be glad when I can set up the altar at home. I keep thinking about how it was in the beginning for Sensei when he moved to Santa Fe. Trials and tribulations, trying to do the impossible among ignorant people he was surrounded with. I remember his great courage, then and now; his great faith in what he was supposed to be doing. He is a great example for me, even though it's not exactly the same detail. There is an amazing amount of similarity. He paved the way so I can walk this path, too. Life would have been meaningless for me were I not been given the knowledge of how to find the truth. Everything else in the pursuit of petty ego gratification is without any real satisfaction.

At least I always knew that but I didn't know what else there was, what other way to move. I am here for all those seekers of the truth who live in Seattle. I want to help them find what they need, as it was shown to me. And to keep on digging deeper in myself.

January 31, 1993. All this obstruction to settle in our home. First having to go to a lawyer to prevent Jake, the seller's agent, from taking the house out from under us. Then get out the tenants who were living there. The one on Joe's side was served an eviction but the one on my side had said she was leaving so she wasn't served and now she has changed her mind. I'm thinking we should go to his attorney, Windemere, and make a stink and see what can be done. Meanwhile, I have no place to live. Joe has something for a month. I was pretty upset and trying to understand what was happening. I think what we have to do in terms of Futonorito is being obstructed by Kanagi energy. So it's a clash during this transition despite that we have already been redeemed in this time. What helped me see it was the lady on my side was robbed the other night. For the first time in four years, since she has been living there. She didn't really want to stay – it is pushing her out.

I am hoping Jake will be obliged to find her a place to live and pay her first few months' rent. That should convince her to leave even though she is a Section 8, the government is paying most of her rent. This is what occurred to me in meditation. I was sitting there crying, trembling in anger, asking that it be removed from me so I could understand. I am glad I'm feeling sane again and my faith is restored. We must be powerful forces for Futonorito or it wouldn't have been made so hard. I am thinking that if we had bought it in the usual way, we would have had to wait three months for a loan anyway. It would not have been this house, a duplex with everything separate, in a convenient area with a big yard. And affordable.

Meanwhile, I am essentially homeless but feeling optimistic again. It has been up and down and very painful since I arrived on December 4th. I must keep up the courage and not be taken by phenomena.

February 5, 1993. Each morning, as I am waking up, I keep catching myself full of self-criticism. I find the prettiest things to chastise myself with, just looking for things, things that happened so long ago and can't be corrected now and really weren't so terrible. It reflects my anxiety, living under present living conditions. I forget to trust that the difficulties I'm facing will pass and are to be expected at the beginning of a new life chapter. I'm even criticizing myself for talking this way – I hear my brother's voice making fun of me that I have no right to life or any sense of self-esteem and accomplishment, like ordinary mortals. I'm moving into Joe's side of the house tomorrow because so far, that's the only tenant leaving. My side is still up in the air. Very frustrating. I so much want and need my own space, to set up my alter and make sounds, not to feel apologetic about my normal needs or my dogs' presence. It seems like years ago that I lived in my house in Santa Fe and had things the way I liked.

Still, it's no good to suffer over it. Last week I came close to a heart attack when Lisa, the tenant on my side, changed her mind about leaving and I didn't know how to get her out. I was in shock. But it's just another roadblock to Futonorito and the work I must do. Not to take it personally and get sick over it. Not is the time for me to learn about trust and faith and to let go of the illusion of control over things. I don't want to beat myself up about it because I am not in control. Sure is hard living this way, in chaos and in shit, trying to be detached the whole time.

February 17, 1993. Having moved into my house finally, I am completely exhausted. I'm trying to go slow but there is so much to do. At this point, I have no choice but to slow down because I ache from head to foot and I am on the verge of getting sick. This house will be very nice once it's done. After all, it had been rehabilitated from years of neglect and abuse. Still, I am feeling happy and hopeful. There was such a pall hanging over me in Santa Fe from all the misery and heartbreak of the years spent with HKL's painful deterioration and death. There was no way to lift it except by changing my space altogether. Better to look forward to new things and retrieve me. How could I have sacrificed it to circumstance and internalized pressure to do things, "right."

"Right." In this society, it always means wrong for my spirit and freedom. To nurture what is sacred and essential to my life is always asked to be sacrificed, otherwise, it's called selfish. Finally, in my old age, I'm seeing through it. Let me have the strength and clarity not to let myself be betrayed again – ever. I think it's a false idea of dependency that starts the self-betrayal, where the inner child is still thinking it has to control its world by pleasing the grow-ups or else it won't survive. Always self-betrayal is based on fear. This whole society is run on fear. But then I get insight into its modus vivendi it loses its power over me. That this should happen so late in the game is another device. Ordinarily, at this stage, I would be dead or on medication, clouding my vision or in some kind of dependent position. Or totally out of society in some kind of convent or "home." Very few escape and that I am so fortunate is because of this way of healing that Sensei found. A healing method that has come back to us.

It gives me hope for the future of humanity. Beginning here with Kototama practice, however, few we are, it has begun. It seems as if our genes were programmed to wake up after a ten-thousand-year sleep, and some of us have the sense already. I'm thinking of Penny who can't get out of her robot mentality, no matter how long she has been with Sensei. Her darkness was so powerful it always managed to throw a shadow on my light, sooner or later. And so many others. The age of the robot-self is so powerful it reflects the grip this society can still manage to exert. The hook is always fear, the child's fear of being undone. And the symbolism of blood. The bloody sacrifice, spilling away my life on meaningless activity. I must remember this. To follow my way no matter what. Even not to be afraid that Sensei will mistakenly abandon me. Only a child can be abandoned. I have to have the faith for my life to trust in being free.

I must tell Joe not to be a slave to the house. Here is his opportunity to perform his music and he needs the time to practice, so he and Darren can perform well. I hope he and Marcelle will have the courage. The house will always be there, waiting to be done. Just to make it livable, so they can move in.

March 5, 1993. I was trying to read the class notes from 1978 and it made me sick. Not so much what he was saying but it reminded me of how the school turned into a nightmare with all the dishonesty and arrogance. All my rage and indignation came back with the memories. The students and faculty only understood how to play the game with him and never heard what he was saying about Kototama and how to be a real healer. That was too much for them to understand. It seemed the school's demise would be certain. Sensei is still trying in his way. But he refuses to teach Kototama anymore.

I relived all the humiliation I endured and lack of recognition for my work there. I was determined to learn, to study the Kototama and therapy with him because there was no one else to teach it to me. I was determined. Perhaps his difficult attitude was a device, I'm trying to continue searching this Inori method from the hints he's given me, and to go deeper into the sounds. I feel I will get there but the inner knowledge is slow in unraveling. I can wait and be thankful for my task. Any other kind of work is miserable and meaningless to me. It was always like that, from my teenage years. I couldn't understand how people could live the way they do. How can they be happy? Oh yes, for a moment, like when you fall in love or make more money or some fame comes. This is not what I call happiness and a sense of life being "right." It is a privilege, in spite of the hardships in my life, to be pursuing this truth. Nothing less will do.

If I were to marry again, it would only obstruct my path, I would have to concentrate on him more and I would lose my way. Not to be some man's slave again.

March 6, 1993. I was getting scared because nothing was being done about converting the VA mortgage loan at 11% to a bank loan at 4.5% or so. Joe didn't even appear at the first meeting with the bank. He had good reason, but still, my inner nine-year-old child was feeling abandoned. I have a really hard night. Waves of panic kept me from sleeping. Yesterday, we went together and put it through tentatively in case we should find a better deal elsewhere. Then the good news. Someone is willing to buy his business. He wants to go into just hauling by himself with occasional help from Marselle or a hired man. This will make his life much easier, giving him more time for music, and he will be free of the partnership. Darren was causing him all kinds of aggravation whenever it was his turn at running the business and Joe would have to take up the slack. I am concerned that I still have only one patient and not one response from the ads. I keep paying out to Sensei and the landlord and the reserves are dwindling. What will happen if this goes on?

I took a chance in coming here and I have to trust it was the right move. I wonder what else I can do to attract patients. What am I not doing? Is there something wrong with my spirit? I believe in what I am doing and I cannot cave in to fear. I'm asking the universe to help me, to guide me, and to send me patients. Yes, I am really asking. Unlike when we had the restaurant and thought we shouldn't be asking for customers.

Little did I know the HKL was sending out energy to keep them away, now I am really asking for the patients. I have no qualms about that. My work is a blessing for me and them. So how do I let them find me? At what point do I cut back on expenses, like asking Sensei to defer my membership payments as he had done for others? I have to keep on trusting, in the universe and the truth of my work. I'll just keep on going for now and see what happens.

March 19, 1993. I seem to be opening up to the sounds a little more. It's hard to know if it's my present state or the actual differences or maybe there is no difference. They are me and I'm alive and changing all the time. Still, there would be some consistency, I'm still scratching at them. I read again about the god-woman Omuro Hime, otherwise known as Roma, who married Moses, Moses Romulus. These are in Takeuti documents, they record how they founded Rome. This is a little after Moses "disappeared" from Sinai and returned to Hinomoto, marrying Roma. Moses at this time becomes a god-man, too. She is something of a role model for me at this time. I think of my relationship with Sensei and how I can't have a relationship with him that feels right. As long as we are so n-equal. Something about Roma, who could be a god-woman.

I suppose what I am saying is that perhaps I can develop far enough to not feel inferior with Sensei when he acts so obnoxiously controlling and humiliating. I wouldn't take him so seriously and just laugh at him, he would like that too. As it is, I still overreact to the mere sound of his voice, scolding or kindly, whichever way. The only way I can feel more confident is if it were real, that I was in a more open place in my consciousness. I don't think I really want anything else. Always there are intellectual and emotional hurdles there, but practice does make a difference. A little encouragement helps. Like the gratification, I felt when Darren was so taken with my concrete poetry when I showed it to him. No one in Santa Fe has such sensitivity or openness to new experiences. Perhaps the Seattle atmosphere is freer. I feel freer here, and I'll not worry so much that I'm not making a living yet. I know it will come and I'm not a deluded fool to think so.

March 29, 1993. There is a sense of panic again and feeling queer inside. I am so much by myself with no friends to talk to. It feels queer to be talking to myself all the time. I'm doing good work with myself, using this quiet time well. But I'm so scared today, it's coming from my early upbringing. I was left alone so much and I felt I would go mad at times. No one was sympathetic or even noticed. I managed to cope but it left its mark. As an adult, I am no longer afraid of it and I use my time well.

But not today. That abandoned child needs to be heard and felt. So I'll talk about fear and loneliness. I certainly expected it when I planned to move. How much can I ask Joe to be there for me? It's just today. I am feeling glum and discouraged. What is happening to my practice and how do I make it happen? It is a time of trial. Yet I am growing spiritually.

Perhaps it is because of these days of waiting, I find that I have to reassure my inner child that it is ok to be doing this. I am learning more about Inori diagnosis as well as the treatment methods. To step into that space is realizing a dream, however strange that it is to my childhood identity. I would have been afraid of someone like me. That's why I have been cut off from my relatives, even those with education. And that's why it is a lonely path, to practice the Kototama. It just isn't understandable to most people and I am only learning as a student. But to study this was is not the norm and I have to recognize it. It is a courageous thing to do, and I am up to it. But somehow, today, I don't want to be feeling so lonely. What sort of friends can I have? If I has more patients it would be a kind of external proof of my validity. At least Joe encourages me and sees how difficult it is.

It will be better later, I have faith this time will pass and I'll be better for it. It isn't for nothing. Now I'm feeling better and not so scared. I need to review this moment in my life from time to time and keep my perspective. It seems to me that I can make friends through my patients, when that happens, at least it will be something. To keep my sense of humor and not to hear some old grown-up's voice laughing at me, I am playing a different game. Getting out of the old program to find my real self.

April 10, 1993. I caught myself feeling angry and judgmental of my daughter-in-law because she looked so contented, sitting in her chair watching TV. Now, why was I so unreasonable when I love and admire this young woman? As if she had no right to be happy. I realized I was recalling my early family experience, my mother disapproving of any satisfaction that I might feel. It was threatening to her sense of control over me and that I could be a separate entity from her. I could be happy and without including her, and further, happiness was something that only she could give to me. Unfortunately, we didn't have the same values. Her childish pursuit of material things and status for me was too superficial and empty. We were really so different in our personal needs but any sense of separation would cause her to panic.

So there I was, recalling her personality, hearing her angry voice, criticizing me, undermining any self-esteem that I might have on my own. I wasn't aware of it, I wasn't allowed to be happy, and I wasn't good enough without her direction. So I chose ways that wouldn't bring me happiness, I was relating to people that guaranteed a miserable outcome. I thought that was called "being serious." I believe moving to Seattle is my attempt at trying to create a life of satisfaction. A chance to have a busy practice. It seemed so hopeless in Santa Fe. I was tired of Sensei treating me like a second-class student, and I had no hope of changing that attitude. Even now, unless I do very well here, he will certainly not change his mind.

I felt that he could never appreciate the person that I am. However, it works out, at least I can make an independent life without feeling I am so much under his thumb. Distance is a blessing. I have a right to be my own person, unencumbered by his dependency. It is impossible to have an intimate relationship with him. I looked straight into his eyes once, to see who he really is, and he looked back at me with anger at my temerity.

April 20, 1993. The Waco religious fanatics all died in a fire they set themselves, obeying their leader. Ninety-five people, including 17 children all died on this day. Their cult leader was described by a psychiatrist as arrogant, selfish, manipulative, and unscrupulous. He used his control over his worshipful followers to gratify his ego-mania. It made me feel very uneasy. Why did following such a person answer their inner religious or spiritual need? A need so powerful and one I could really identify with, at least in years past. But the experience is still recent enough. It makes me cry for them because I know what they were searching for so desperately and how easily I, too, could have been conned. I wonder about it sometimes to this day. There is something of me and Sensei here, his ego-mania and my blindly following him. But we both had grace, not to entirely fall into that. He is much bigger than his weaknesses and maybe I was protected, somehow.

He kept telling us this is not a religion and we must find it in ourselves and not look to him for the answers as an easy way. We must keep searching inside because we all have it as part of our human constitution. It is a matter of waking up what we already know. Bless him for his strength and integrity.

And still, there is some doubt, and that is what's upsetting to me. I look at what's going on in Paris with Akenhiko and the dojo they recently constructed, based on the Ise shrine in Japan. And there was Sensei in his white kimono, hitting the gong at their opening ceremonies.

He said he would never go back there again. It seems he had been tempted, and fell in this time. He knew that some of the French people who showed heightened religious sensitivity would contrast his attendance of the ceremony as another form of religion. The Americans understood the Kototama Institute as a religion, too. But they didn't buy into him but just gave him lip service as a means to attain their own agenda. I can't believe how easy it is to give in to temptation along the way, to use the psychic power that develops to practice for small ego acts. I remember my patient asked me about his girlfriend. Asked me to synchronize with her spirit to give him an answer. What misuses of this healing, I felt so sick to have given in like that, it was a mistake that I won't make again.

Actually, in my relationships, there was always something unspoken, hidden, and insincere and I am wondering if that is typical of a dysfunctional society. People are too afraid at their core to be really open with others, perhaps even with themselves.

I too have played this game, ignoring the lie and feelings of dissatisfaction. My relationships have always been disappointing. But being optimistic, I can go on searching, in myself to at least be honest with myself.   I can't depend on what other people do. It's enough to not participate in it from my end. It is a difficult road but a happy one as I get past each hurdle along the way and catch those fleeting thoughts that are crucial to self-understanding before I bury them.

May 3, 1993. Who do I resist telling my story? Feelings of panic in my stomach, fear of reprisal to speak the truth.   I called this banker about refinancing our mortgage.   He was so angry with me for daring to ask a straightforward question as if a mere woman was not allowed, as if it were not my money and my responsibility. I felt sick as if this child had no business to ask anything.   And he, the bank clerk, needed the power of money so badly that he could pretend it was his own money that he was disbursing. I suddenly felt my life was hopeless. All my striving to have a life of freedom and personal integrity was doomed. I began recalling Sensei's harsh treatment of me and the times he would freely give information to everyone else but I had to find out accidentally. It made me feel second-rate. Perhaps he, too, has a power problem and abused me in order to staunch his feelings of inferiority. One can do this with wives and lovers. I was reliving the old resentment fiercely.

And darling Joe, I told him what happened about my conversation with the clerk. He called the abusive clerk and abused him. He acted very angrily. 'What's this about my loan?!?' He had the man bowing and scraping and then told Joe told him it was ok, that Robin, our contact had already explained everything satisfactorily. Unfortunately, Robin, gives Joe better treatment than me, taking him more seriously than this old lady. But most importantly, when I lost it with the clerk, I could find my sanity again by going back to my substance and staying there until I could create myself anew and come out whole. There is no other way to recover from the pain except by going back to my source and coming out again. It's the only way for all of us to heal from this material age. It is not enough to compensate with money or to escape spiritually. That doesn't change the state of the disease. It's only temporary relief from the symptoms.

We have to go back to the source and recreate ourselves constantly. I believe this is happening all the time but without any consciousness, so we continue the sick pattern instead of getting out of the program. We should be born again, over and over with each breath we take. It is thanks to Joe's spirit that I can live and do my work here in Seattle like this. I don't have to back down.

May 31, 1993. Putting the pieces together, getting some perspective now on my life of the past 20 years, my relationships with my husband and my Sensei most of all, seeing people's egos, men in particular. Looking at how I played my part in complying, thinking they must be right somehow, and ignoring the reality I could see for myself. I am working my way out of that, trying to be a better judge. I saw this holy woman, "the Mother." I spoke with her, mind to mind, she knows there is something more but doesn't want to seek any further. She is quite content where she is, in a state of religious bliss, doing good works. She was annoyed I could suggest anything else. But is it enough to save thousands when there are billions of people on the planet that are suffering? Everyone looks for a savior and has no idea of their own responsibility. In a way she saves them to continue doing this kind of society, not to be enlightened, as she claims. They wait to get zapped by her hug. Like Jesus, she gives them spiritual nourishment to keep them going for a while longer. And I could see she has no fear at all. Just this side of madness to have no fear. One needn't apologize about having fear, which is normal. One needs the courage to deal with life.

I met some friends of DeeDee's. Melinda and another lady I liked. But this Dean, who I also met, is completely insane and on an ego trip. His pulses showed great disturbance and his big blue eyes were obviously over-expanded. I believe he drinks up people's energy. When I got home and went to bed, I was tossing and turning all night and in the morning, I woke up late and felt hungover. Only now I am starting to recover, after treating myself for kidney energy replenishment, I realized that I must learn to guard myself against such a person. Perhaps I must face this vampire, looking him straight into his big eyes and even attack him rather than falling back to a defensive position. Interesting, I am starting to meet people in Seattle.

The Courage Between The Lines

Epilogue.

The line between courage and cowardice is a lot thinner than most people would believe. Anyone who has been feeling this way would recognize themselves in this. And most people wouldn't care to admit it. It takes courage to look inside yourself. And even more, courage to write it for other people to see. I'm proud of you mom.   I have given this writing a lot of thought. In my mind I realize that parents take on an exaggerated role for their children, my mother was the Madonna and never wrong although I had a hard time understanding her and found myself repelled by the Kototama as something that would always show my faults and because of that, I could never attain the "truth" intuitively. Even if I wanted to. I needed something more concrete in my life. This vague language that didn't have its basis on anything that I could understand became just another entanglement and besides going to college became my next enterprise.

The feelings that exerted themselves on me as I read through this were like reliving a part of my history that I felt angrier about than I had realized. I was constantly reminding myself that my story was not the road that my mother took. I read the definition of Stockholm Syndrome, and its meaning is a sensitive description of victims who are being held captive, developing feelings of sympathy towards the captor over the length of time held in captivity. I don't mean to suggest that I completely understand the varieties of feelings that I have learned about through my mother's writings. I do understand that she was a very complicated woman, and perhaps symbolic of a deeper conflict rooted in a family experiencing the history of the American immigrant, she and her brother were the first-generation Americans in her family. Her family life spanned American history during a depression, a world war, and several other conflicts, the cold war, civil rights, and other social injustices. I believe this experience profoundly created a perfect storm of conflict that no one simple behavioral definition could encompass.

In some measure, there were rays of sunlight and hope in her life and she was brilliant to seek out help to understand the struggles of her emotional personal history. It seems for her this journey could not really come to a completion. I think she was battling her monsters up until the end when she passed away from cancer. However, I pause and remember what she said about her understanding of the future of humanity.

"It gives me hope for the future of humanity. Beginning here with Kototama practice, however, few we are, it has begun. It seems as if our genes were programmed to wake up after a ten-thousand-year sleep and some of us have the sense already. The age of the robot-self is so powerful it reflects the grip this society can still manage to exert. The hook is always fear, the child's fear of being undone. And the symbolism of blood. The bloody sacrifice, spilling away my life on meaningless activity."

This vision had come from a surprising source. To my mind, someone who had so much to work through in life would only be, and possible could only be, expected to try to reach out for their own improvement. A personal reality filled with fear, horror, and sacrifice, one would only be expected to concentrate on behavioral health improvement at a personal level and beyond that would be exceptional. I could describe her as an artist that never had the chance to be professional but that would not be entirely true, she did much in her field for women to help improve women's social and political standing.

She headed up the first women's caucus in New York and through that birthed the Women's Liberation Movement. She was involved in many political rallies that changed our world and improved it. But she also knew the isolation of being a housewife and the impossible expectations of being a wife during a period where society stifled the creativity of women and expected them to cater to the men that they married.

In part, this is a story of a woman whose dream to be a creative soul had to take many turns and that brought on many frustrations. However, she was successful in looking into life with creative flair and always brought her experiences into her job and made her position unique. In New York, she worked as an art teacher at Greenwich House, an organization dedicated to helping at-risk youth. In New Mexico, she worked at the Kototama Institute and was one of the founding members there. She help to bring about the production and documentation of so many articles, lectures, and books that her teacher, Sensei Mikoto Masahilo Nakazono, authored. And with that started again to produce art and poetry in Santa Fe, starting with a modest portrait she painted of my brother and me during our teen years. She was just beginning to show in local galleries when she thought about moving to Seattle, Washington. She really never had the opportunity to produce more artwork as she continued her journey of self-improvement and pursued her ideas of healing others through natural medicine.

She loved Washington so much.

She had the heart "of a humble wildflower."

Dave Farbrook

About the Author

Sarai in front of her painting at Concepts Gallery Santa Fe, NM 1993.

Sarai (a.k.a. Sara Saporta) was born in New York City, in 1930 to David and Victoria Saporta, who manufactured clothing. She grew up in Manhattan. She had one sibling, who is now retired and living in Illinois. She graduated from The Cooper Union for the Advancement of Science and Art, she began her career, then married Carl Fernbach-Flarsheim in 1960, and devoted her energy to raising her children. However, in New York, she involved herself with other artists, and taught art to at-risk youth at the Greenwich House Youth Community Center, in New York. Later, in 1971, moved to New Mexico with her family and became an Acupuncturist. Later she returned to her first love of painting and writing. She appeared briefly at Concepts Gallery on Canyon Road, Santa Fe NM.

Her artwork in what could be termed expressionistic followed her philosophical beliefs. The elements of expressionism had to defend themselves to her style and transformed into a whole new realm of art that imitates sound and vibration. She eventually moved to Sedro Woolley, WA, where she died at age 65.

Books where her works can be found:

A Documentary HerStory of Women Artists in Revolution: Compilation of documents – newspaper articles, editorials, correspondences between museum officials, flyers, writings, and manifestos – by Women Artists in Revolution (W.A.R.) from 1969 to 1971.

About the Editor

Dave F. Farbrook is currently living in Albuquerque, New Mexico. With over 25 years of professional experience in research, has compiled a rich anthology of his father's accomplishments and conclusions. And now publishing this book of his mother's journal writings.

He has authored essays, a cookbook, edited 4 books written by Carl Fernbach-Flarsheim, has a blog site, and as of this publication, broadcasts with Albuquerque NOW! Podcast.

Additionally, he has edited 4 children's empowerment books with JJ Alexander. He has assisted with grant writing for several non-profit organizations in urban improvement and STEM/MSAP education.

He has been blessed with a daughter and a son, both are very successful in their areas of interest.

Discover The Stories That You Never Knew
Published by: Dave Mysite Dot Com

C Est le Numéro 3 D'Approches: The Conceptual Typewriter
October 24, 2021, Paperback $12.00 US
Carl Fernbach-Flarsheim (Author), Dave F Farbrook (Editor).
The Conceptual Typewriter program for the computer display unit, teletype, and button console. The programming instructions for the conceptual typewriter are for developing sequential display of symbols that creates a hierarchy of labels.

D P R: A progression of a life trajectory
October 17, 2021, Paperback $14.79 US
Carl Fernbach-Flarsheim (Author), Dave F Farbrook (Editor).
Carl Fernbach-Flarsheim, the stories, the short poem, and the letter that describes a progression of thoughts and reactions to experiences, and memories, a life trajectory that brought a sense of completion in one artist's life and hopefully opens the door to a new generation to consider the behavior of the human mind, the physical and the spiritual.

The Five Books Of Moses: "A covenant with myself and with all those that are between: I bring the war to a close."
October 11, 2021, Paperback $19.95 US
HiKaLu (aka Carl Fernbach-Flarsheim) (Author), Dave F Farbrook (Editor).
Carl Fernbach-Flarsheim, under his Sage Name HiKaLu, is an interpretation of the Five Old Testament scrolls referred to as the Pentateuch. He wrote this book in part to bring the memories of war within himself to a close and based his ideas in part on what he learned through his teacher Sensei Mazahilo Nakazono.

A Play For Puppets: A Play in Three Acts Paperback.
August 17, 2021, Paperback $7.65 US
HiKaLu (aka Carl Fernbach-Flarsheim) (Author), Dave F Farbrook (Editor).
"Play for Puppets" which Carl Fernbach-Flarsheim also drew the illustrations, is filled with axioms, pointed comments about the state of the world, it is humorous, but sometimes very serious. It could be said that the play has sound bytes that seem to have roots in existentialism. But the principles of the sounds and the order of perception described in the Second and Third Civilizations can clearly be observed in the characters he brought to life in the play.